Against the Heathen (Contra Gentiles)
St. Athanasius

Table of Contents:

Against the Heathen (Contra Gentiles)

Section 1: Introduction

The purpose of the book a vindication of Christian doctrine, and especially of the Cross, against the scoffing objection of Gentiles. The effects of this doctrine its main vindication. The knowledge of our religion and of the truth of things is independently manifest rather than in need of human teachers, for almost day by day it asserts itself by facts, and manifests itself brighter than the sun by the doctrine of Christ. 2. Still, as you nevertheless desire to hear about it, Macarius[1], come let us as we may be able set forth a few points of the faith of Christ: able though you are to find it out from the divine oracles, but yet generously desiring to hear from others as well. 3. For although the sacred and inspired Scriptures are sufficient [2] to declare the truth,– while there are other works of our blessed teachers [3] compiled for this purpose, if he meet with which a man will gain some knowledge of the interpretation of the Scriptures, and be able to learn what he wishes to know,–still, as we have not at present in our hands the compositions of our teachers, we must communicate in writing to you what we learned from them,–the faith, namely, of Christ the Saviour; lest any should

---

[1] See de Incarn. 1 and note there.

[2] Constantly insisted on by Athan. Cf. de Incarn. 5, and note on de Decr. 32.

[3] De Incarn. 56. 2; he may also be referring to works from the Alex. school, such as Orig. de Princ.

hold cheap the doctrine taught among us, or think faith in Christ unreasonable. For this is what the Gentiles traduce and scoff at, and laugh loudly at us, insisting on the one fact of the Cross of Christ; and it is just here that one must pity their want of sense, because when they traduce the Cross of Christ they do not see that its power has filled all the world, and that by it the effects of the knowledge of God are made manifest to all. 4. For they would not have scoffed at such a fact, had they, too, been men who genuinely gave heed to His divine Nature. On the contrary, they in their turn would have recognised this man as Saviour of the world, and that the Cross has been not a disaster, but a healing of Creation. 5. For if after the Cross all idolatry was overthrown, while every manifestation of demons is driven away by this Sign [4], and Christ alone is worshipped and the Father known through Him, and, while gainsayers are put to shame, He daily invisibly wins over the souls of these gainsayers [5],–how, one might fairly ask them, is it still open to us to regard the matter as human, instead of confessing that He Who ascended the Cross is Word of God and Saviour of the World? But these men seem to me quite as bad as one who should traduce the sun when covered by clouds, while yet wondering at his light, seeing how the whole of creation is illumined by him. 6. For as the light is noble, and the sun, the chief cause of light, is nobler still, so, as it is a divine thing for the whole world to be

---

[4] Cf. de Incarn. 47. 2, 48. 3, Vit. Ant. passim.
[5] Cf. de Incarn. 50. 3, 51. 3, &c.

filled with his knowledge, it follows that the orderer and chief cause of such an achievement is God and the Word of God. 7. We speak then as lies within our power, first refuting the ignorance of the unbelieving; so that what is false being refuted, the truth may then shine forth of itself, and that you yourself, friend, may be reassured that you have believed what is true, and in coming to know Christ have not been deceived. Moreover, I think it becoming to discourse to you, as a lover of Christ, about Christ, since I am sure that you rate faith in and knowledge of Him above anything else whatsoever.

Section 2

S:2. Evil no part of the essential nature of things. The original creation and constitution of man in grace and in the knowledge of God. In the beginning wickedness did not exist. Nor indeed does it exist even now in those who are holy, nor does it in any way belong to their nature. But men later on began to contrive it and to elaborate it to their own hurt. Whence also they devised the invention of idols, treating what was not as though it were.2. For God Maker of all and King of all, that has His Being beyond [6] all substance and human discovery, inasmuch as He is good and exceeding noble, made, through His own Word our Saviour Jesus Christ, the human race after His own image, and constituted man able to see and know realities by means of this assimilation to Himself, giving him also a conception [7] and knowledge even of His own eternity, in order that, preserving his nature intact, he might not ever either depart from his idea of God, nor recoil from the communion of the holy ones; but having the grace of Him that gave it, having also God's own power from the Word of the Father, he might rejoice and have fellowship with the Deity, living the life of immortality unharmed and truly blessed. For having nothing to hinder his knowledge of the Deity, he ever beholds, by his purity, the Image of the Father, God the Word, after Whose image he

---

[6] See Orig. c. Cels. vii. 42 sqq. de Princ. I. 1.
[7] Restored in Christ, see S:34.

himself is made. He is awe-struck as he contemplates that Providence [8] which through the Word extends to the universe, being raised above the things of sense and every bodily appearance, but cleaving to the divine and thought-perceived things in the heavens by the power of his mind. 3. For when the mind of men does not hold converse with bodies, nor has mingled with it from without aught of their lust, but is wholly above them, dwelling with itself as it was made to begin with, then, transcending the things of sense and all things human, it is raised up on high; and seeing the Word, it sees in Him also the Father of the Word, taking pleasure in contemplating Him, and gaining renewal by its desire toward Him; 4. exactly as the first of men created, the one who was named Adam in Hebrew, is described in the Holy Scriptures as having at the beginning had his mind to God-ward in a freedom unembarrassed by shame, and as associating with the holy ones in that contemplation of things perceived by the mind which he enjoyed in the place where he was—the place which the holy Moses called in figure a Garden. So purity of soul is sufficient of itself to reflect God, as the Lord also says, "Blessed are the pure in heart, for they shall see God."

---

[8] Cf. Ep. AEg. 15, Apol. Fug. passim, Orat. iii. 37.

Section 3

S:3. The decline of man from the above condition, owing to his absorption in material things. Thus then, as we have said, the Creator fashioned the race of men, and thus meant it to remain. But men, making light of better things, and holding back from apprehending them, began to seek in preference things nearer to themselves. 2. But nearer to themselves were the body and its senses; so that while removing their mind from the things perceived by thought, they began to regard themselves; and so doing, and holding to the body and the other things of sense, and deceived as it were in their own surroundings, they fell into lust of themselves, preferring what was their own to the contemplation of what belonged to God. Having then made themselves at home in these things, and not being willing to leave what was so near to them, they entangled their soul with bodily pleasures, vexed and turbid with all kind of lusts, while they wholly forgot the power they originally had from God. 3. But the truth of this one may see from the man who was first made, according to what the holy Scriptures tell us of him. For he also, as long as he kept his mind to God, and the contemplation of God, turned away from the contemplation of the body. But when, by counsel of the serpent, he departed from the consideration of God, and began to regard himself, then they not only fell to bodily lust, but knew that they were naked, and knowing, were ashamed. But they knew that they were naked, not so much of clothing as that they were become stripped of the contemplation of divine things, and had transferred their understanding to the contraries. For having departed from the consideration of the one and the true, namely, God, and from desire of Him, they had thenceforward embarked in divers lusts and in those of the several bodily senses. 4. Next, as is apt to happen, having formed a desire for each and sundry, they began to be habituated to these desires, so that they were even afraid to leave them: whence the soul became subject to cowardice and alarms, and pleasures and thoughts of mortality. For not being willing to leave her lusts, she fears death and her separation from the body. But again, from lusting, and not meeting with gratification, she learned to commit murder and wrong. We are then led naturally to shew, as best we can, how she does this.

Section 4

S:4. The gradual abasement of the Soul from Truth to Falsehood by the abuse of her freedom of Choice. Having departed from the contemplation of the things of thought, and using to the full the several activities of the body, and being pleased with the contemplation of the body, and seeing that pleasure is good for her, she was misled and abused the name of good, and thought that pleasure was the very essence of good: just as though a man out of his mind and asking for a sword to use against all he met, were to think that soundness of mind. 2. But having fallen in love with pleasure, she began to work it out in various ways. For being by nature mobile, even though she have turned away from what is good, yet she does not lose her mobility. She moves then, no longer according to virtue or so as to see God, but imagining false things, she makes a novel use of her power, abusing it as a means to the pleasures she has devised, since she is after all made with power over herself. 3. For she is able, as on the one hand to incline to what is good, so on the other to reject it; but in rejecting the good she of course entertains the thought of what is opposed to it, for she cannot at all cease from movement, being, as I said before, mobile by nature. And knowing her own power over herself, she sees that she is able to use the members of her body in either direction, both toward what is, or toward what is not. 4. But good is, while evil is not; by what is, then, I mean what is good, inasmuch as it has its pattern in God Who is. But by what is not

I mean what is evil, in so far as it consists in a false imagination in the thoughts of men. For though the body has eyes so as to see Creation, and by its entirely harmonious construction to recognise the Creator; and ears to listen to the divine oracles and the laws of God; and hands both to perform works of necessity and to raise to God in prayer; yet the soul, departing from the contemplation of what is good and from moving in its sphere, wanders away and moves toward its contraries. 5. Then seeing, as I said before, and abusing her power, she has perceived that she can move the members of the body also in an opposite way: and so, instead of beholding the Creation, she turns the eye to lusts, shewing that she has this power too; and thinking that by the mere fact of moving she is maintaining her own dignity, and is doing no sin in doing as she pleases; not knowing that she is made not merely to move, but to move in the right direction. For this is why an apostolic utterance assures us "All things are lawful, but not all things are expedient [9]."

---

[9] 1 Cor. x. 23.

Section 5

S:5. Evil, then consists essentially in the choice of what is lower in preference to what is higher. But the audacity of men, having regard not to what is expedient and becoming, but to what is possible for it, began to do the contrary; whence, moving their hands to the contrary, it made them commit murder, and led away their hearing to disobedience, and their other members to adultery instead of to lawful procreation; and the tongue, instead of right speaking, to slander and insult and perjury; the hands again, to stealing and striking fellow-men; and the sense of smell to many sorts of lascivious odours; the feet, to be swift to shed blood, and the belly to drunkenness and insatiable gluttony [10]. 2. All of which things are a vice and sin of the soul: neither is there any cause of them at all, but only the rejection of better things. For just as if a charioteer [11], having mounted his chariot on the race-course, were to pay no attention to the goal, toward which he should be driving, but, ignoring this, simply were to drive the horse as he could, or in other words as he would, and often drive against those he met, and often down steep places, rushing wherever he impelled himself by the speed of the team, thinking that thus running he has not missed the goal,–for he regards the running only, and does not see that he has passed wide of the goal;–so the soul too, turning from the way toward God, and

---

[10] Rom. iii. 10 foll.
[11] Cf. Plato Phaedrus 246 C, 248 A, 253 E, 254.

10

driving the members of the body beyond what is proper, or rather, driven herself along with them by her own doing, sins and makes mischief for herself, not seeing that she has strayed from the way, and has swerved from the goal of truth, to which the Christ-bearing man, the blessed Paul, was looking when he said, "I press on toward the goal unto the prize of the high calling of Christ Jesus [12]:" so that the holy man, making the good his mark, never did what was evil.

---

[12] Phil. iii. 14.

Section 6

S:6. False views of the nature of evil: viz., that evil is something in the nature of things, and has substantive existence. (a) Heathen thinkers: (evil resides in matter). Their refutation. (b) Heretical teachers: (Dualism). Refutation from Scripture. Now certain of the Greeks, having erred from the right way, and not having known Christ, have ascribed to evil a substantive and independent existence. In this they make a double mistake: either in denying the Creator to be maker of all things, if evil had an independent subsistence and being of its own; or again, if they mean that He is maker of all things, they will of necessity admit Him to be maker of evil also. For evil, according to them, is included among existing things. 2. But this must appear paradoxical and impossible. For evil does not come from good, nor is it in, or the result of, good, since in that case it would not be good, being mixed in its nature or a cause of evil. 3. But the sectaries, who have fallen away from the teaching of the Church, and made shipwreck concerning the Faith [13], they also wrongly think that evil has a substantive existence. But they arbitrarily imagine another god besides the true One, the Father of our Lord Jesus Christ, and that he is the unmade producer of evil and the head of wickedness, who is also artificer of Creation. But these men one can easily refute, not only from the divine Scriptures, but also from the human understanding itself, the very source of these their

---

[13] 1 Tim. i. 19.

insane imaginations. 4. To begin with, our Lord and Saviour Jesus Christ says in His own gospels confirming the words of Moses: "The Lord God is one," and "I thank thee, Father, Lord of heaven and earth[14]." But if God is one, and at the same time Lord of heaven and earth, how could there be another God beside Him? or what room will there be for the God whom they suppose, if the one true God fills all things in the compass of heaven and earth? or how could there be another creator of that, whereof, according to the Saviour's utterance, the God and Father of Christ is Himself Lord? 5. Unless indeed they would say that it were, so to speak, in an equipoise, and the evil god capable of getting the better of the good God. But if they say this, see to what a pitch of impiety they descend. For when powers are equal, the superior and better cannot be discovered. For if the one exist even if the other will it not, both are equally strong and equally weak equally, because the very existence of either is a defeat of the other's will: weak, because what happens is counter to their wills: for while the good God exists in spite of the evil one, the evil god exists equally in spite of the good.

---

[14] Mark xii. 29; Matt. xi. 25.

Section 7

S:7. Refutation of dualism from reason. Impossibility of two Gods. The truth as to evil is that which the Church teaches: that it originates, and resides, in the perverted choice of the darkened soul. More especially, they are exposed to the following reply. If visible things are the work of the evil god, what is the work of the good God? for nothing is to be seen except the work of the Artificer. Or what evidence is there that the good God exists at all, if there are no works of His by which He may be known? for by his works the artificer is known. 2. Or how could two principles exist, contrary one to another: or what is it that divides them, for them to exist apart? For it is impossible for them to exist together, because they are mutually destructive. But neither can the one be included in the other, their nature being unmixed and unlike. Accordingly that which divides them will evidently be of a third nature, and itself God. But of what nature could this third something be? good or evil? It will be impossible to determine, for it cannot be of the nature of both. 3. This conceit of theirs, then, being evidently rotten, the truth of the Church's theology must be manifest: that evil has not from the beginning been with God or in God, nor has any substantive existence; but that men, in default of the vision of good, began to devise and imagine for themselves what was not, after their own pleasure. 4. For as if a man, when the sun is shining, and the whole earth illumined by his light, were to shut fast his eyes and imagine

14

darkness where no darkness exists, and then walk wandering as if in darkness, often falling and going down steep places, thinking it was dark and not light,–for, imagining that he sees, he does not see at all;–so, too, the soul of man, shutting fast her eyes, by which she is able to see God, has imagined evil for herself, and moving therein, knows not that, thinking she is doing something, she is doing nothing. For she is imagining what is not, nor is she abiding in her original nature; but what she is is evidently the product of her own disorder. 5. For she is made to see God, and to be enlightened by Him; but of her own accord in God's stead she has sought corruptible things and darkness, as the Spirit says somewhere in writing, "God made man upright, but they have sought out many inventions [15]." Thus it has been then that men from the first discovered and contrived and imagined evil for themselves. But it is now time to say how they came down to the madness of idolatry, that you may know that the invention of idols is wholly due, not to good but to evil. But what has its origin in evil can never be pronounced good in any point,–being evil altogether.

---

[15] Eccl. vii. 29.

Section 8

S:8. The origin of idolatry is similar. The soul, materialised by forgetting God, and engrossed in earthly things, makes them into gods. The race of men descends into a hopeless depth of delusion and superstition. Now the soul of mankind, not satisfied with the devising of evil, began by degrees to venture upon what is worse still. For having experience of diversities of pleasures, and girt about with oblivion of things divine; being pleased moreover and having in view the passions of the body, and nothing but things present and opinions about them, ceased to think that anything existed beyond what is seen, or that anything was good save things temporal and bodily; so turning away and forgetting that she was in the image of the good God, she no longer, by the power which is in her, sees God the Word after whose likeness she is made; but having departed from herself, imagines and feigns what is not. 2. For hiding, by the complications of bodily lusts, the mirror which, as it were, is in her, by which alone she had the power of seeing the Image of the Father, she no longer sees what a soul ought to behold, but is carried about by everything, and only sees the things which come under the senses. Hence, weighted with all fleshly desire, and distracted among the impressions of these things, she imagines that the God Whom her understanding has forgotten is to be found in bodily and sensible things, giving to things seen the name of God, and glorifying only those things which she desires and which are pleasant to her eyes. 3. Accordingly, evil is the cause which brings idolatry in its train; for men, having learned to contrive evil, which is no reality in itself, in like manner feigned for themselves as gods beings that had no real existence. Just, then, as though a man had plunged into the deep, and no longer saw the light, nor what appears by light, because his eyes are turned downwards, and the water is all above him; and, perceiving only the things in the deep, thinks that nothing exists beside them, but that the things he sees are the only true realities; so the men of former time, having lost their reason, and plunged into the lusts and imaginations of carnal things, and forgotten the knowledge and glory of God, their reasoning being dull, or rather following unreason, made gods for themselves of things seen, glorifying the creature rather than the Creator [16], and deifying the works rather than the Master, God, their Cause and Artificer. 4. But just as, according to the above simile, men who plunge into the deep, the deeper they go down, advance into darker and deeper places, so it is with mankind. For they did not keep to idolatry in a simple form, nor did they abide in that with which they began; but the longer they went on in their first condition, the more new superstitions they invented: and, not satiated with the first evils, they again filled themselves. with others, advancing further in utter shamefulness, and surpassing themselves in impiety. But to this the divine Scripture testifies when it says, "When the

---

[16] Rom. i. 25.

wicked cometh unto the depth of evils, he despiseth [17]."

Section 9

S:9. The various developments of idolatry:
worship of the heavenly bodies, the elements,
natural objects, fabulous creatures, personified
lusts, men living and dead. The case of Antinous,
and of the deified Emperors. For now the
understanding of mankind leaped asunder from
God; and going lower in their ideas and
imaginations, they gave the honour due to God
first to the heaven and the sun and moon and the
stars, thinking them to be not only gods, but also
the causes of the other gods lower than themselves
[18]. Then, going yet lower in their dark
imaginations, they gave the name of gods to the
upper aether and the air and the things in the air.
Next, advancing further in evil, they came to
celebrate as gods the elements and the principles
of which bodies are composed, heat and cold and
dryness and wetness. 2. But just as they who have
fallen flat creep in the slime like land-snails, so the
most impious of mankind, having fallen lower
and lower from the idea of God, then set up as
gods men, and the forms of men, some still living,
others even after their death. Moreover,
counselling and imagining worse things still, they
transferred the divine and supernatural name of
God at last even to stones and stocks, and

---

[18] For the following chapters Doellinger, The Gentile and
the Jew,', is a rich mine of illustration. The recently
published Manual of the History of Religions,' by Prof.
Chantepie de la Saussaye (Eng. Tra. pub. by Longmans),
summarises the best results of recent research.

creeping things both of land and water, and irrational wild beasts, awarding to them every divine honour, and turning from the true and only real God, the Father of Christ. 3. But would that even there the audacity of these foolish men had stopped short, and that they had not gone further yet in impious self-confusion. For to such a depth have some fallen in their understanding, to such darkness of mind, that they have even devised for themselves, and made gods of things that have no existence at all, nor any place among things created. For mixing up the rational with the irrational, and combining things unlike in nature, they worship the result as gods, such as the dog-headed and snake-headed and ass-headed gods among the Egyptians, and the ram-headed Ammon among the Libyans. While others, dividing apart the portions of men's bodies, head, shoulder, hand, and foot, have set up each as gods and deified them, as though their religion were not satisfied with the whole body in its integrity. 4. But others, straining impiety to the utmost, have deified the motive of the invention of these things and of their own wickedness, namely, pleasure and lust, and worship them, such as their Eros, and the Aphrodite at Paphos. While some of them, as if vying with them in depravation, have ventured to erect into gods their rulers or even their sons, either out of honour for their princes, or from fear of their tyranny, such as the Cretan Zeus, of such renown among them, and the Arcadian Hermes; and among the Indians Dionysus, among the Egyptians Isis and Osiris and Horus, and in our own time Antinous,

favourite of Hadrian, Emperor of the Romans,
whom, although men know he was a mere man,
and not a respectable man, but on the contrary,
full of licentiousness, yet they worship for fear of
him that enjoined it. For Hadrian having come to
sojourn in the land of Egypt, when Antinous the
minister of his pleasure died, ordered him to be
worshipped; being indeed himself in love with the
youth even after his death, but for all that offering
a convincing exposure of himself, and a proof
against all idolatry, that it was discovered among
men for no other reason than by reason of the lust
of them that imagined it. According as the
wisdom of God testifies beforehand when it says,
"The devising of idols was the beginning of
fornication[19]." 5. And do not wonder, nor think
what we are saying hard to believe, inasmuch as it
is not long since, even if it be not still the case that
the Roman Senate vote to those emperors who
have ever ruled them from the beginning, either
all of them, or such as they wish and decide, a
place among the gods, and decree them to be
worshipped [20] . For those to whom they are
hostile, they treat as enemies and call men,
admitting their real nature, while those who are
popular with them they order to be worshipped
on account of their virtue, as though they had it
in their own power to make gods, though they are

---

[19] Wisd. xiv. 12.
[20] Constantine was the last Emperor officially deified
(D.C.B., I. 649), but even Theodosius is raised to heaven by
the courtly Claudian Carm. de 111 Cons. Honor. 163 sqq.;
cf. Gwatkin, p. 54, note.

themselves men, and do not profess to be other than mortal. 6. Whereas if they are to make gods, they ought to be themselves gods; for that which makes must needs be better than that which it makes, and he that judges is of necessity in authority over him that is judged, while he that gives, at any rate that which he has, confers a layout, just as, of course, every king, in giving as a favour what he has to give, is greater and in a higher position than those who receive. If then they decree whomsoever they please to be gods, they ought first to be gods themselves. But the strange thing is this, that they themselves by dying as men, expose the falsehood of their own vote concerning those deified by them.

Section 10

S:10. Similar human origin of the Greek gods, by decree of Theseus. The process by which mortals became deified. But this custom is not a new one, nor did it begin from the Roman Senate: on the contrary, it had existed previously from of old, and was formerly practised for the devising of idols. For the gods renowned from of old among the Greeks, Zeus, Poseidon, Apollo, Hephaestus, Hermes, and, among females, Hera and Demeter and Athena and Artemis, were decreed the title of gods by the order of Theseus, of whom Greek history tells us [21].; and so the men who pass such decrees die like men and are mourned for, while those in whose favour they are passed are worshipped as gods. What a height of inconsistency and madness! knowing who passed the decree, they pay greater honour to those who are the subjects of it. 2. And would that their idolatrous madness had stopped short at males, and that they had not brought down the title of deity to females. For even women, whom it is not safe to admit to deliberation about public affairs, they worship and serve with the honour due to God, such as those enjoined by Theseus as above stated, and among the Egyptians[22] Isis and the

---

[21] This is probably a reference to the hiera anagraphe of Euhemerus, which Christian apologists commonly took as genuine history: see S:12, note 1

[22] Cf. de la Saussaye, S:51. Isis, as goddess of the earth, corresponded to Demeter; as goddess of the dead, to the Kore (Persephone).

Maid and the Younger one [23], and among others Aphrodite. For the names of the others I do not consider it modest even to mention, full as they are of all kind of grotesqueness. 3. For many, not only in ancient times but in our own also, having lost their beloved ones, brothers and kinsfolk and wives; and many women who had lost their husbands, all of whom nature proved to be mortal men, made representations of them and devised sacrifices, and consecrated them; while later ages, moved by the figure and the brilliancy of the artist, worshipped them as gods, thus falling into inconsistency with nature [24] . For whereas their parents had mourned for them, not regarding them as gods (for had they known them to be gods they would not have lamented them as if they had perished; for this was why they represented them in an image, namely, because they not only did not think them gods, but did not believe them to exist at all, and in order that the sight of their form in the image might console them for their being no more), yet the foolish people pray to them as gods and invest them with the honour of the true God. 4. For example, in Egypt, even to this day, the death-dirge is

---

[23] The Neotera is a puzzle. The most likely suggestion is that of Montfaucon, who refers it to Cleopatra, who nea Isis echrematize (Plut. Vit. Anton.). He cites also a coin of M. Antony, on which Cleopatra is figured as thea neotera. Several such are given by Vaillant, de Numism. Cleopatr. 189. She was not the first of her name to adopt this style, see Head Hist. Num. pp. 716, 717. The text might be rendered Isis, both the Maid and the Younger.'

[24] Cf. Wisd. xiv. 12 sqq. quoted below.

celebrated for Osiris and Horus and Typho and the others. And the caldrons[25] at Dodona, and the Corybantes in Crete, prove that Zeus is no god but a man, and a man born of a cannibal father. And, strange to say, even Plato, the sage admired among the Greeks, with all his vaunted understanding about God, goes down with Socrates to Peiraeus to worship Artemis, a figment of man's art.[26]

---

[25] Cf. Greg. Naz. Or. v 32, p. 168 c, and Dict. G. and R. Geog. I. p. 783a.
[26] Plat. Rep. I. ad init.

Section 11

S:11. The deeds of heathen deities, and particularly of Zeus. But of these and such like inventions of idolatrous madness, Scripture taught us beforehand long ago, when it said [27] , "The devising of idols was the beginning of fornication, and the invention of them, the corruption of life. For neither were they from the beginning, neither shall they be for ever. For the vainglory of men they entered into the world, and therefore shall they come shortly to an end. For a father afflicted with untimely mourning when he hath made an image of his child soon taken away, now honoured him as a god which was then a dead man, and delivered to those that were under him ceremonies and sacrifices. Thus in process of time an ungodly custom grown strong was kept as a law. And graven images were worshipped by the commands of kings. Whom men could not honour in presence because they dwelt afar off, they took the counterfeit of his visage from afar, and made an express image of the king whom they honoured, to the end that by this their forwardness they might flatter him that was absent as if he were present. Also the singular diligence of the artificer did help to set forward the ignorant to more superstition: for he, peradventure, willing to please one in authority, forced all his skill to make the resemblance of the best fashion: and so the multitude, allured by the grace of the work, took him now for a god, which a little before was but

---

[27] Wisd. xiv. 12 sqq.

honoured as a man: and this was an occasion to deceive the world, for men serving either calamity or tyranny, did ascribe unto stones and stocks the incommunicable Name." 2. The beginning and devising of the invention of idols having been, as Scripture witnesses, of such sort, it is now time to shew thee the refutation of it by proofs derived not so much from without as from these men's own opinions about the idols. For to begin at the lowest point, if one were to take the actions of them they call gods, one would find that they were not only no gods, but had been even of men the most contemptible. For what a thing it is to see the loves and licentious actions of Zeus in the poets! What a thing to hear of him, on the one hand carrying off Ganymede and committing stealthy adulteries, on the other in panic and alarm lest the walls of the Trojans should be destroyed against his intentions! What a thing to see him in grief at the death of his son Sarpedon, and wishing to succour him without being able to do so, and, when plotted against by the other so-called gods, namely, Athena and Hera and Poseidon, succoured by Thetis, a woman, and by AEgaeon of the hundred hands, and overcome by pleasures, a slave to women, and for their sakes running adventures in disguises consisting of brute beasts and creeping things and birds; and again, in hiding on account of his father's designs upon him, or Cronos bound by him, or him again mutilating his father! Why, is it fitting to regard as a god one who has perpetrated such deeds, and who stands accused of things which not even the public laws of the Romans allow those to do who are merely men?

Section 12

S:12. Other shameful actions ascribed to heathen deities. All prove that they are but men of former times, and not even good men. For, to mention a few instances out of many to avoid prolixity, who that saw his lawless and corrupt conduct toward Semele, Leda, Alcmene, Artemis, Leto, Maia, Europe, Danae, and Antiope, or that saw what he ventured to take in hand with regard to his own sister, in having the same woman as wife and sister, would not scorn him and pronounce him worthy of death? For not only did he commit adultery, but he deified and raised to heaven those born of his adulteries, contriving the deification as a veil for his lawlessness: such as Dionysus, Heracles, the Dioscuri, Hermes, Perseus, and Soteira. 2. Who, that sees the so-called gods at irreconcileable strife among themselves at Troy on account of the Greeks and Trojans, will fail to recognise their feebleness, in that because of their mutual jealousies they egged on even mortals to strife? Who, that sees Ares and Aphrodite wounded by Diomed, or Hera and Aidoneus from below the earth, whom they call a god, wounded by Heracles, Dionysus by Perseus, Athena by Arcas, and Hephaestus hurled down and going lame, will not recognise their real nature, and, while refusing to call them gods, be assured (when he hears that they are corruptible and passible) that they are nothing but men [28], and feeble men too, and admire those that inflicted the wounds rather than the wounded? 3. Or who that sees the adultery of Ares with Aphrodite, and Hephaestus contriving a snare for the two, and the other so-called gods called by Hephaestus to view the adultery, and coming and seeing their licentiousness, would not laugh and recognise their worthless character? Or who would not laugh at beholding the drunken folly and misconduct of Heracles toward Omphale? For their deeds of pleasure, and their unconscionable loves, and their divine images in gold, silver, bronze, iron, stone, and wood, we need not seriously expose by argument, since the facts are abominable in themselves, and are enough taken alone to furnish proof of the deception; so that one's principal feeling is pity for those deceived about them. 4. For, hating the adulterer who tampers with a wife of their own, they are not ashamed to deify the teachers of adultery; and refraining from incest themselves they worship those who practise it; and admitting that the corrupting of children is an evil, they serve those who stand accused of it and do not blush to

---

[28] This explanation of gods as deified men is known as Euhemerism, from Euhemerus, who broached the theory in the third century, b.c. (supra, 10, note 1); but there were Euhemerists in Greece before Euhemerus' (Jowett's Plato, 2. 101). The Fathers very commonly adopt the theory, for which, however, there are very slight grounds. Such cases as those of Antinous and the Emperors, as well as the legends of heroes and demigods, gave it some plausibility (see Doellinger; Gentile and Jew, vol. i. p. 344, Eng. Tr.).

ascribe to those they call gods things which the laws forbid to exist even among men.

Section 13

S:13. The folly of image worship and its dishonour to art. Again, in worshipping things of wood and stone, they do not see that, while they tread under foot and burn what is in no way different, they call portions of these materials gods. And what they made use of a little while ago, they carve and worship in their folly, not seeing, nor at all considering that they are worshipping, not gods, but the carver's art. 2. For so long as the stone is uncut and the wood unworked, they walk upon the one and make frequent use of the other for their own purposes, even for those which are less honourable. But when the artist has invested them with the proportions of his own skill, and impressed upon the material the form of man or woman, then, thanking the artist, they proceed to worship them as gods, having bought them from the carver at a price. Often, moreover, the image-maker, as though forgetting the work he has done himself, prays to his own productions, and calls gods what just before he was paring and chipping. 3. But it were better, if need to admire these things, to ascribe it to the art of the skilled workman, and not to honour productions in preference to their producer. For it is not the material that has adorned the art, but the art that has adorned and deified the material. Much juster were it, then, for them to worship the artist than his productions, both because his existence was prior to that of the gods produced by art, and because they have come into being in the form he pleased to give them.

But as it is, setting justice aside, and dishonouring skill and art, they worship the products of skill and art, and when the man is dead that made them, they honour his works as immortal, whereas if they did not receive daily attention they would certainly in time come to a natural end. 4. Or how could one fail to pity them in this also, in that seeing, they worship them that cannot see, and hearing, pray to them that cannot hear, and born with life and reason, men as they are, call gods things which do not move at all, but have not even life, and, strangest of all, in that they serve as their masters beings whom they themselves keep under their own power? Nor imagine that this is a mere statement of mine, nor that I am maligning them; for the verification of all this meets the eyes, and whoever wishes to do so may see the like.

Section 14

S:14. Image worship condemned by Scripture. But better testimony about all this is furnished by Holy Scripture, which tells us beforehand when it says [29], "Their idols are silver and gold, the work of men's hands. Eyes have they and will not see; a mouth have they and will not speak; ears have they and will not hear; noses have they and will not smell; hands have they and will not handle; feet have they and will not walk; they will not speak through their throat. Like unto them be they that make them." Nor have they escaped prophetic censure; for there also is their refutation, where the Spirit says [30], "they shall be ashamed that have formed a god, and carved all of them that which is vain: and all by whom they were made are dried up: and let the deaf ones among men all assemble and stand up together, and let them be confounded and put to shame together; for the carpenter sharpened iron, and worked it with an adze, and fashioned it with an auger, and set it up with the arm of his strength: and he shall hunger and be faint, and drink no water. For the carpenter chose out wood, and set it by a rule, and fashioned it with glue, and made it as the form of a man and as the beauty of man, and set it up in his house, wood which he had cut from the grove and which the Lord planted, and the rain gave it growth that it might be for men to burn, and that he might take thereof and warm

---

[29] Ps. cxv. 5 sqq.
[30] Isa. xliv. 9 sqq. (LXX.).

himself, and kindle, and bake bread upon it, but the residue they made into gods, and worshipped them, the half whereof they had burned in the fire. And upon the half thereof he roasted flesh and ate and was filled, and was warmed and said: It is pleasant to me, because I am warmed and have seen the fire.' But the residue thereof he worshipped, saying, Deliver me for thou art my god.' They knew not nor understood, because their eyes were dimmed that they could not see, nor perceive with their heart; nor did he consider in his heart nor know in his understanding that he had burned half thereof in the fire, and baked bread upon the coals thereof, and roasted flesh and eaten it, and made the residue thereof an abomination, and they worship it. Know that their heart is dust and they are deceived, and none can deliver his soul. Behold and will ye not say, There is a lie in my right hand?'" 2. How then can they fail to be judged godless by all, who even by the divine Scripture are accused of impiety? or how can they be anything but miserable, who are thus openly convicted of worshipping dead things instead of the truth? or what kind of hope have they? or what kind of excuse could be made for them, trusting in things without sense or movement, which they reverence in place of the true God?

Section 15

S:15. The details about the gods conveyed in the representations of them by poets and artists shew that they are without life, and that they are not gods, nor even decent men and women. For would that the artist would fashion the gods even without shape, so that they might not be open to so manifest an exposure of their lack of sense. For they might have cajoled the perception of simple folk to think the idols had senses, were it not that they possess the symbols of the senses, eyes for example and noses and ears and hands and mouth, without any gesture of actual perception and grasp of the objects of sense. But as a matter of fact they have these things and have them not, stand and stand not, sit and sit not. For they have not the real action of these things, but as their fashioner pleased, so they remain stationary, giving no sign of a god, but evidently mere inanimate objects, set there by man's art. 2. Or would that the heralds and prophets of these false gods, poets I mean and writers, had simply written that they were gods, and not also recounted their actions as an exposure of their godlessness and scandalous life. For by the mere name of godhead they might have filched away the truth, or rather have caused the mass of men to err from the truth. But as it is, by narrating the loves and immoralities of Zeus, and the corruptions of youths by the other gods, and the voluptuous jealousies of the females, and the fears and acts of cowardice and other wickednesses, they merely convict themselves of narrating not merely about no gods, but not even about respectable men, but on the contrary, of telling tales about shameful persons far removed from what is honourable.

Section 16

S:16. Heathen arguments in palliation of the above: and (1) the poets are responsible for these unedifying tales.' But are the names and existence of the gods any better authenticated? Both stand or fall together. Either the actions must be defended or the deity of the gods given up. And the heroes are not credited with acts inconsistent with their nature, as, on this plea, the gods are. But perhaps, as to all this, the impious will appeal to the peculiar style of poets, saying that it is the peculiarity of poets to feign what is not, and, for the pleasure of their hearers, to tell fictitious tales; and that for this reason they have composed the stories about gods. But this pretext of theirs, even more than any other, will appear to be superficial from what they themselves think and profess about these matters. 2. For if what is said in the poets is fictitious and false, even the nomenclature of Zeus, Cronos, Hera, Ares and the rest must be false. For perhaps, as they say, even the names are fictitious, and, while no such being exists as Zeus, Cronos, or Ares, the poets feign their existence to deceive their hearers. But if the poets feign the existence of unreal beings, how is it that they worship them as though they existed? 3. Or perhaps, once again, they will say that while the names are not fictitious, they ascribe to them fictitious actions. But even this is equally precarious as a defence. For if they made up the actions, doubtless also they made up the names, to which they attributed the actions. Or if they tell the truth about the names, it follows that they tell the truth about the actions too. In particular, they who have said in their tales that these are gods certainly know how gods ought to act, and would never ascribe to gods the ideas of men, any more than one would ascribe to water the properties of fire; for fire burns, whereas the nature of water on the contrary is cold. 4. If then the actions are worthy of gods, they that do them must be gods; but if they are actions of men, and of disreputable men, such as adultery and the acts mentioned above, they that act in such ways must be men and not gods. For their deeds must correspond to their natures, so that at once the actor may be made known by his act, and the action may be ascertainable from his nature. So that just as a man discussing about water and fire, and declaring their action, would not say that water burned and fire cooled, nor, if a man were discoursing about the sun and the earth, would he say the earth gave light, while the sun was sown with herbs and fruits, but if he were to say so would exceed the utmost height of madness, so neither would their writers, and especially the most eminent poet of all, if they really knew that Zeus and the others were gods, invest them with such actions as shew them to be not gods, but rather men, and not sober men. 5. Or if, as poets, they told falsehoods, and you are maligning them, why did they not also tell falsehoods about the courage of the heroes, and feign feebleness in the place of courage, and courage in that of feebleness? For they ought in that case, as with Zeus and Hera, so also to slanderously accuse Achilles of want of courage, and to celebrate the might of Thersites, and, while charging Odysseus with dulness, to make out Nestor a reckless person, and to narrate effeminate actions of Diomed and Hector, and manly deeds of Hecuba. For the fiction and falsehood they ascribe to the poets ought to extend to all cases. But in fact, they kept the truth for their men, while not ashamed to tell falsehoods about their so-called gods. 6. And as some of them might argue, that they are telling falsehoods about their licentious actions, but that in their praises, when they speak of Zeus as father of gods, and as the highest, and the Olympian, and as reigning in heaven, they are not inventing but speaking truthfully; this is a plea which not only myself, but anybody can refute. For the truth will be clear, in opposition to them, if we recall our previous proofs. For while their actions prove them to be men, the panegyrics upon them go beyond the nature of men. The two things then are mutually inconsistent; for neither is it the nature of heavenly beings to act in such ways, nor can any one suppose that persons so acting are gods.

Section 17

S:17. The truth probably is, that the scandalous
tales are true, while the divine attributes ascribed
to them are due to the flattery of the poets. What
inference then is left to us, save that while the
panegyrics are false and flattering, the actions told
of them are true? And the truth of this one can
ascertain by common practice. For nobody who
pronounces a panegyric upon anyone accuses his
conduct at the same time, but rather, if men's
actions are disgraceful, they praise them up with
panegyrics, on account of the scandal they cause,
so that by extravagant praise they may impose
upon their hearers, and hide the misconduct of
the others. 2. Just as if a man who has to
pronounce a panegyric upon someone cannot find
material for it in their conduct or in any personal
qualities, on account of the scandal attaching to
these, he praises them up in another manner,
flattering them with what does not belong to
them, so have their marvellous poets, put out of
countenance by the scandalous actions of their so-
called gods, attached to them the superhuman
title, not knowing that they cannot by their
superhuman fancies veil their human actions, but
that they will rather succeed in shewing, by their
human shortcomings, that the attributes of God
do not fit them. 3. And I am disposed to think
that they have recounted the passions and the
actions of the gods even in spite of themselves.
For since they were endeavouring to invest with
what Scripture calls the incommunicable name

and honour of[31] God them that are no gods but mortal men, and since this venture of theirs was great and impious, for this reason even against their will they were forced by truth to set forth the passions of these persons, so that their passions recorded in the writings concerning them might be in evidence for all posterity as a proof that they were no gods.

---

[31] Wisd. xiv. 21. Cf. Isa. xlii. 8, and xlviii. 11

Section 18

S:18. Heathen defence continued. (2) The gods are worshipped for having invented the Arts of Life.' But this is a human and natural, not a divine, achievement. And why, on this principle, are not all inventors deified? What defence, then, what proof that these are real gods, can they offer who hold this superstition? For, by what has been said just above, our argument has demonstrated them to be men, and not respectable men. But perhaps they will turn to another argument, and proudly appeal to the things useful to life discovered by them, saying that the reason why they regard them as gods is their having been of use to mankind. For Zeus is said to have possessed the plastic art, Poseidon that of the pilot, Hephaestus the smith's, Athena that of weaving, Apollo that of music, Artemis that of hunting, Hera dressmaking, Demeter agriculture, and others other arts, as those who inform us about them have related. 2. But men ought to ascribe them and such like arts not to the gods alone but to the common nature of mankind, for by observing nature [32] men discover the arts. For even common parlance calls art an imitation of nature. If then they have been skilled in the arts they pursued, that is no reason for thinking them gods, but rather for thinking them men; for the arts were not their creation, but in them they, like others, imitated nature. 3. For men having a natural capacity for knowledge according to the

---

[32] phusis is here used in a double sense.

43

definition laid down[33] concerning them, there is nothing to surprise us if by human intelligence, and by looking of themselves at their own nature and coming to know it, they have hit upon the arts. Or if they say that the discovery of the arts entitles them to be proclaimed as gods, it is high time to proclaim as gods the discoverers of the other arts on the same grounds as the former were thought worthy of such a title. For the Phoenicians invented letters, Homer epic poetry, Zeno of Elea dialectic, Corax of Syracuse rhetoric, Aristaeus bee-keeping, Triptolemus the sowing of corn, Lycurgus of Sparta and Solon of Athens laws; while Palamedes discovered the arrangement of letters, and numbers, and measures and weights. And others imparted various other things useful for the life of mankind, according to the testimony of our historians. 4. If then the arts make gods, and because of them carved gods exist, it follows, on their shewing, that those who at a later date discovered the other arts must be gods. Or if they do not deem these worthy of divine honour, but recognise that they are men, it were but consistent not to give even the name of gods to Zeus, Hera, and the others, but to believe that they too have been human beings, and all the more so, inasmuch as they were not even respectable in their day; just as by the very fact of sculpturing their form in statues they shew that they are nothing else but men.

---

[33] By Aristotle, Top. V. ii.-iv. where man is defined as zoon epistemes dektikon: compare Metaph. I. i. All men by nature desire to know.'

Section 19

S:19. The inconsistency of image worship.
Arguments in palliation. (1) The divine nature
must be expressed in a visible sign. (2) The image
a means of supernatural communications to men
through angels. For what other form do they give
them by sculpture but that of men and women
and of creatures lower yet and of irrational nature,
all manner of birds, beasts both tame and wild,
and creeping things, whatsoever land and sea and
the whole realm of the waters produce? For men
having fallen into the unreasonableness of their
passions and pleasures, and unable to see anything
beyond pleasures and lusts of the flesh, inasmuch
as they keep their mind in the midst of these
irrational things, they imagined the divine
principle to be in irrational things, and carved a
number of gods to match the variety of their
passions. 2. For there are with them images of
beasts and creeping things and birds, as the
interpreter of the divine and true religion says,
"They became vain in their reasonings, and their
senseless heart was darkened. Professing
themselves to be wise, they became fools, and
changed the glory of the incorruptible God for the
likeness of an image of corruptible man, and of
birds and four-footed beasts and creeping things,
wherefore God gave them up unto vile passions."
For having previously infected their soul, as I said
above, with the irrationalities of pleasures, they
then came down to this making of gods; and,
once fallen, thenceforward as though abandoned

45

in their rejection of God, thus they wallow[34] in them, and portray God, the Father of the Word, in irrational shapes. 3. As to which those who pass for philosophers and men of knowledge[35] among the Greeks, while driven to admit that their visible gods are the forms and figures of men and of irrational objects, say in defence that they have such things to the end that by their means the deity may answer them and be made manifest; because otherwise they could not know the invisible God, save by such statues and rites. 4. While those[36] who profess to give still deeper and more philosophical reasons than these say, that the reason of idols being prepared and fashioned is for the invocation and manifestation of divine angels and powers, that appearing by these means they may teach men concerning the knowledge of God; and that they serve as letters for men, by referring to which they may learn to apprehend God, from the manifestation of the divine angels effected by their means. Such then is their

---

[34] Cf. Orat. iii. 16.

[35] This may refer to Maximus of Tyre (Saussaye, S:11), or to the lost treatise of the divine Iamblichus' Peri agalmaton, which was considered worth answering by Christian writers as late as the seventh century (Philoponus in Phot. Bibl. Cod. 215).

[36] This is in effect the defence of the Scriptor de Mysteriis' (possibly Iamblichus, see Bernays 2 Abhandlungen' 1880, p. 37): material means of worship are a means of access directly to the lower (or quasi-material) gods, and so indirectly to the higher. Few men can reach the latter without the aid of their manifestation in the lower; parestin a& 204;los tois enulois ta a& 203;la (v. 23, cf. 14).

mythology,—for far be it from us to call it a theology. But if one examine the argument with care, he will find that the opinion of these persons also, not less than that of those previously spoken of, is false.

Section 20

S:20. But where does this supposed virtue of the image reside? in the material, or in the form, or in the maker's skill? Untenability of all these views. For one might reply to them, bringing the case before the tribunal of truth, How does God make answer or become known by such objects? Is it due to the matter of which they consist, or to the form which they possess? For if it be due to the matter, what need is there of the form, instead of God manifesting Himself through all matter without exception before these things were fashioned? And in vain have they built their temples to shut in a single stone, or stock, or piece of gold, when all the world is full of these substances. 2. But if the superadded form be the cause of the divine manifestation, what is the need of the material, gold and the rest, instead of God manifesting Himself by the actual natural animals of which the images are the figures? For the opinion held about God would on the same principle have been a nobler one, were He to manifest Himself by means of living animals, whether rational or irrational, instead of being looked for in things without life or motion. 3. Wherein they commit the most signal impiety against themselves. For while they abominate and turn from the real animals, beasts, birds, and creeping things, either because of their ferocity or because of their dirtiness, yet they carve their forms in stone, wood, or gold, and make them gods. But it would be better for them to worship the living things themselves, rather than to worship their figures in stone. 4. But perhaps neither is the case, nor is either the material or the form the cause of the divine presence, but it is only skilful art that summons the deity, inasmuch as it is an imitation of nature. But if the deity communicates with the inmates on account of the art, what need, once more, of the material, since the art resides in the men? For if God manifests Himself solely because of the art, and if for this reason the images are worshipped as gods, it would be right to worship and serve the men who are masters of the art, inasmuch as they are rational also, and have the skill in themselves.

Section 21

S:21. The idea of communications through angels involves yet wilder inconsistency, nor does it, even if true, justify the worship of the image. But as to their second and as they say profounder defence, one might reasonably add as follows. If these things are made by you, ye Greeks, not for the sake of a self-manifestation of God Himself, but for the sake of a presence there of angels, why do you rank the images by which ye invoke the powers as superior and above the powers invoked? For ye carve the figures for the sake of the apprehension of God, as ye say, but invest the actual images with the honour and title of God, thus placing yourselves in a profane position. 2. For while confessing that the power of God transcends the littleness of the images, and for that reason not venturing to invoke God through them, but only the lesser powers, ye yourselves leap over these latter, and have bestowed on stocks and stones the title of Him, whose presence ye feared, and call them gods instead of stones and men's workmanship, and worship them. For even supposing them to serve you, as ye falsely say, as letters for the contemplation of God, it is not right to give the signs greater honour than that which they signify. For neither if a man were to write the emperor's name would it be without risk to give to the writing more honour than to the emperor; on the contrary, such a man incurs the penalty of death; while the writing is fashioned by the skill of the writer. 3. So also yourselves, had ye your reasoning power in full strength, would not reduce to matter so great a revelation of the Godhead: but neither would ye have given to the image greater honour than to the man that carved it. For if there be any truth in the plea that, as letters, they indicate the manifestation of God, and are therefore, as indications of God, worthy to be deified, yet far more would it be right to deify the artist who carved and engraved them, as being far more powerful and divine than they, inasmuch as they were cut and fashioned according to his will. If then the letters are worthy of admiration, much more does the writer exceed them in wonder, by reason of his art and the skill of his mind. If then it be not fitting to think that they are gods for this reason, one must again interrogate them about the madness concerning the idols, demanding from them the justification for their being in such a form.

Section 22

S:22. The image cannot represent the true form of God, else God would be corruptible. For if the reason of their being thus fashioned is, that the Deity is of human form, why do they invest it also with the forms of irrational creatures? Or if the form of it is that of the latter, why do they embody it also in the images of rational creatures? Or if it be both at once, and they conceive God to be of the two combined, namely, that He has the forms both of rational and of irrational, why do they separate what is joined together, and separate the images of brutes and of men, instead of always carving it of both kinds, such as are the fictions in the myths, Scylla, Charybdis, the Hippocentaur, and the dog-headed Anubis of the Egyptians? For they ought either to represent them solely of two natures in this way, or, if they have a single form, not to falsely represent them in the other as well. 2. And again, if their forms are male, why do they also invest them with female shapes? Or if they are of the latter, why do they also falsify their forms as though they were males? Or if again they are a mixture of both, they ought not to be divided, but both ought to be combined, and follow the type of the so-called hermaphrodites, so that their superstition should furnish beholders with a spectacle not only of impiety and calumny, but of ridicule as well. 2. And generally, if they conceive the Deity to be corporeal, so that they contrive for it and represent belly and hands and feet, and neck also, and breasts and the other organs that go to make man, see to what impiety and godlessness their mind has come down, to have such ideas of the Deity. For it follows that it must be capable of all other bodily casualties as well, of being cut and divided, and even of perishing altogether. But these and like things are not properties of God, but rather of earthly bodies. 3. For while God is incorporeal and incorruptible, and immortal, needing nothing for any purpose, these are both corruptible, and are shapes of bodies, and need bodily ministrations, as we said before [37] . For often we see images which have grown old renewed, and those which time, or rain, or some or other of the animals of the earth have spoiled, restored. In which connexion one must condemn their folly, in that they proclaim as gods things of which they themselves are the makers, and themselves ask salvation of objects which they themselves adorn with their arts to preserve them from corruption, and beg that their own wants may be supplied by beings which they well know need attention from themselves, and are not ashamed to call lords of heaven and all the earth creatures whom they shut up in small chambers.

---

[37] Supra xiii. 3.

Section 23

S:23. The variety of idolatrous cults proves that they are false. But not only from these considerations may one appreciate their godlessness, but also from their discordant opinions about the idols themselves. For if they be gods according to their assertion and their speculations, to which of them is one to give allegiance, and which of them is one to judge to be the higher, so as either to worship God with confidence, or as they say to recognise the Deity by them without ambiguity? For not the same beings are called gods among all; on the contrary, for every nation almost there is a separate god imagined. And there are cases of a single district and a single town being at internal discord about the superstition of their idols. 2. The Phoenicians, for example, do not know those who are called gods among the Egyptians, nor do the Egyptians worship the same idols as the Phoenicians have. And while the Scythians reject the gods of the Persians, the Persians reject those of the Syrians. But the Pelasgians also repudiate the gods in Thrace, while the Thracians know not those of Thebes. The Indians moreover differ from the Arabs, the Arabs from the Ethiopians, and the Ethiopians from the Arabs in their idols. And the Syrians worship not the idols of the Cilicians, while the Cappadocian nation call gods beings different from these. And while the Bithynians have adopted others, the Armenians have imagined others again. And what need is there for me to multiply examples? The men on the continent worship other gods than the islanders, while these latter serve other gods than those of the main lands. 3. And, in general, every city and village, not knowing the gods of its neighbours, prefers its own, and deems that these alone are gods. For concerning the abominations in Egypt there is no need even to speak, as they are before the eyes of all: how the cities have religions which are opposite and incompatible, and neighbours always make a point of worshipping the opposite of those next to them [38] : so much so that the crocodile, prayed to by some, is held in abomination by their neighbours, while the lion, worshipped as a god by others, their neighbours, so far from worshipping, slay, if they find it, as a wild beast; and the fish, consecrated by some people, is used as food in another place. And thus arise fights and riots and frequent occasions of bloodshed, and every indulgence of the passions among them. 4. And strange to say, according to the statement of historians, the very Pelasgians, who learned from the Egyptians the names of the gods, do not know the gods of Egypt, but worship others instead. And, speaking generally, all the nations that are infatuated with idols have

---

[38] Hdt. ii. 69; cf. Juv. Sat. xv. 36, numina vicinorum Odit uterque locus.' This is one of the few places where Athanasius has any Egyptian local colour' (cf. supra 9 and 10). M. Fialon is certainly too imaginative (p. 86 contradicted p. 283), when he sees in the contra Gentes an appreciation of the higher religious principles which the modern science (toute Francaise') of Egyptology has enabled us to read behind the grotesque features of popular Egyptian polytheism.

different opinions and religions, and consistency is not to be met with in any one case. Nor is this surprising. 5. For having fallen from the contemplation of the one God, they have come down to many and diverse objects; and having turned from the Word of the Father, Christ the Saviour of all, they naturally have their understanding wandering in many directions. And just as men who have turned from the sun and are come into dark places go round by many pathless ways, and see not those who are present, while they imagine those to be there who are not, and seeing see not; so they that have turned from God and whose soul is darkened, have their mind in a roving state, and like men who are drunk and cannot see, imagine what is not true.

Section 24

S:24. The so-called gods of one place are used as victims in another. This, then, is no slight proof of their real godlessness. For, the gods for every city and country being many and various, and the one destroying the god of the other, the whole of them are destroyed by all. For those who are considered gods by some are offered as sacrifices and drink-offerings to the so-called gods of others, and the victims of some are conversely the gods of others. So the Egyptians serve the ox, and Apis, a calf, and others sacrifice these animals to Zeus. For even if they do not sacrifice the very animals the others have consecrated, yet by sacrificing their fellows they seem to offer the same. The Libyans have for god a sheep which they call Ammon, and in other nations this animal is slain as a victim to many gods. 2. The Indians worship Dionysus, using the name as a symbol for wine, and others pour out wine as an offering to the other gods. Others honour rivers and springs, and above all the Egyptians pay especial honour to water, calling them gods. And yet others, and even the Egyptians who worship the waters, use them to wash off the dirt from others and from themselves, and ignominiously throw away what is used. While nearly the whole of the Egyptian system of idols consists of what are victims to the gods of other nations, so that they are scorned even by those others for deifying what are not gods, but, both with others and even among themselves, propitiatory offerings and victims.

Section 25

S:25. Human sacrifice. Its absurdity. Its prevalence. Its calamitous results. But some have been led by this time to such a pitch of irreligion and folly as to slay and to offer in sacrifice to their false gods even actual men, whose figures and forms the gods are. Nor do they see, wretched men, that the victims they are slaying are the patterns of the gods they make and worship, and to whom they are offering the men. For they are offering, one may say, equals to equals, or rather, the higher to the lower; for they are offering living creatures to dead, and rational beings to things without motion. 2. For the Scythians who are called Taurians offer in sacrifice to their Virgin, as they call her, survivors from wrecks, and such Greeks as they catch, going thus far in impiety against men of their own race, and thus exposing the savagery of their gods, in that those whom Providence has rescued from danger and from the sea, they slay, almost fighting against Providence; because they frustrate the kindness of Providence by their own brutal character. But others, when they are returned victorious from war, thereupon dividing their prisoners into hundreds, and taking a man from each, sacrifice to Ares the man they have picked out from each hundred. 3. Nor is it only Scythians who commit these abominations on account of the ferocity natural to them as barbarians: on the contrary, this deed is a special result of the wickedness connected with idols and false gods. For the Egyptians used formerly to offer victims of this kind to Hera, and the

Phoenicians and Cretans used to propitiate Cronos in their sacrifices of children. And even the ancient Romans used to worship Jupiter Latiarius, as he was called, with human sacrifices, and some in one way, some in another, but all[39]without exception committed and incurred the pollution: they incurred it by the mere perpetration of the murderous deeds, while they polluted their own temples by filling them with the smoke of such sacrifices. 4. This then was the ready source of numerous evils to mankind. For seeing that their false gods were pleased with these things, they forthwith imitated their gods with like misdoings, thinking that the imitation of superior beings, as they considered them, was a credit to themselves. Hence mankind was thinned by murders of grown men and children, and by licence of all kinds. For nearly every city is full of licentiousness of all kinds, the result of the savage character of its gods; nor is there one of sober life in the idols' temples[40] save only he whose licentiousness is witnessed to by them all[41].

---

[39] On human sacrifice see Saussaye, S:17, and Robertson Smith, Religion of the Semites, pp. 343 sqq., especially p. 347, note 1, for references to examples near the time of this treatise.

[40] Reading eidoleiois conj. Marr.

[41] i.e. among the licentious worshippers the lifeless image is the only one free from vice, although the worshippers credit him with divine attributes, and therefore, according to their superstition, with a licentious life.

Section 26

S:26. The moral corruptions of Paganism all admittedly originated with the gods. Women, for example, used to sit out in old days in the temples of Phoenicia, consecrating to the gods there the hire of their bodies, thinking they propitiated their goddess by fornication, and that they would procure her favour by this. While men, denying their nature, and no longer wishing to be males, put on the guise of women, under the idea that they are thus gratifying and honouring the Mother of their so-called gods. But all live along with the basest, and vie with the worst among themselves, and as Paul said, the holy minister of Christ[42]: "For their women changed the natural use into that which is against nature: and likewise also the men, leaving the natural use of the woman, burned in their lust one toward another, men with men working unseemliness." 2. But acting in this and in like ways, they admit and prove that the life of their so-called gods was of the same kind. For from Zeus they have learned corruption of youth and adultery, from Aphrodite fornication, from Rhea licentiousness, from Ares murders, and from other gods other like things, which the laws punish and from which every sober man turns away. Does it then remain fit to consider them gods who do such things, instead of reckoning them, for the licentiousness of their ways, more irrational than the brutes? Is it fit to consider their worshippers human beings, instead

---

[42] Rom. i. 26.

of pitying them as more irrational than the brutes, and more soul-less than inanimate things? For had they considered the intellectual part of their soul they would not have plunged headlong into these things, nor have denied the true God, the Father of Christ.

Section 27

S:27. The refutation of popular Paganism being
taken as conclusive, we come to the higher form
of nature-worship. How Nature witnesses to God
by the mutual dependence of all her parts, which
forbid us to think of any one of them as the
supreme God. This shewn at length. But perhaps
those who have advanced beyond these things,
and who stand in awe of Creation, being put to
shame by these exposures of abominations, will
join in repudiating what is readily condemned
and refuted on all hands, but will think that they
have a well-grounded and unanswerable opinion,
namely, the worship of the universe and of the
parts of the universe. 2. For they will boast that
they worship and serve, not mere stocks and
stones and forms of men and irrational birds and
creeping things and beasts, but the sun and moon
and all the heavenly universe, and the earth again,
and the entire realm of water: and they will say
that none can shew that these at any rate are not
of divine nature, since it is evident to all, that they
lack neither life nor reason, but transcend even
the nature of mankind, inasmuch as the one
inhabit the heavens, the other the earth. 3. It is
worth while then to look into and examine these
points also; for here, too, our argument will find
that its proof against them holds true. But before
we look, or begin our demonstration, it suffices
that Creation almost raises its voice against them,
and points to God as its Maker and Artificer,
Who reigns over Creation and over all things,
even the Father of our Lord Jesus Christ; Whom

the would-be philosophers turn from to worship and deify the Creation which proceeded from Him, which yet itself worships and confesses the Lord Whom they deny on its account. 4. For if men are thus awestruck at the parts of Creation and think that they are gods, they might well be rebuked by the mutual dependence of those parts; which moreover makes known, and witnesses to, the Father of the Word, Who is the Lord and Maker of these parts also, by the unbroken law of their obedience to Him, as the divine law also says: "The heavens declare the glory of God, and the firmament sheweth His handiwork [43]." 5. But the proof of all this is not obscure, but is clear enough in all conscience to those the eyes of whose understanding are not wholly disabled. For if a man take the parts of Creation separately, and consider each by itself,—as for example the sun by itself alone, and the moon apart, and again earth and air, and heat and cold, and the essence of wet and of dry, separating them from their mutual conjunction,—he will certainly find that not one is sufficient for itself but all are in need of one another's assistance, and subsist by their mutual help. For the Sun is carried round along with, and is contained in, the whole heaven, and can never go beyond his own orbit, while the moon and other stars testify to the assistance given them by the Sun: while the earth again evidently does not yield her crops without rains, which in their turn would not descend to earth without the assistance of the clouds; but not even would the clouds ever

---

[43] Ps. xix. 1.

appear of themselves and subsist, without the air. And the air is warmed by the upper air, but illuminated and made bright by the sun, not by itself. 6. And wells, again, and rivers will never exist without the earth; but the earth is not supported upon itself, but is set upon the realm of the waters, while this again is kept in its place, being bound fast at the centre of the universe. And the sea, and the great ocean that flows outside round the whole earth, is moved and borne by winds wherever the force of the winds dashes it. And the winds in their turn originate, not in themselves, but according to those who have written on the subject, in the air, from the burning heat and high temperature of the upper as compared with the lower air, and blow everywhere through the latter. 7. For as to the four elements of which the nature of bodies is composed, heat, that is, and cold, wet and dry, who is so perverted in his understanding as not to know that these things exist indeed in combination, but if separated and taken alone they tend to destroy even one another according to the prevailing power of the more abundant element? For heat is destroyed by cold if it be present in greater quantity, and cold again is put away by the power of heat, and what is dry, again, is moistened by wet, and the latter dried by the former.

Section 28

S:28. But neither can the cosmic organism be God. For that would make God consist of dissimilar parts, and subject Him to possible dissolution. How then can these things be gods, seeing that they need one another's assistance? Or how is it proper to ask anything of them when they too ask help for themselves one from another? For if it is an admitted truth about God that He stands in need of nothing, but is self-sufficient and self-contained, and that in Him all things have their being, and that He ministers to all rather than they to Him, how is it right to proclaim as gods the sun and moon and other parts of creation, which are of no such kind, but which even stand in need of one another's help? 2. But, perhaps, if divided and taken by themselves, our opponents themselves will admit that they are dependent, the demonstration being an ocular one. But they will combine all together, as constituting a single body, and will say that the whole is God. For the whole once put together, they will no longer need external help, but the whole will be sufficient for itself and independent in all respects; so at least the would-be philosophers will tell us, only to be refuted here once more. 3. Now this argument, not one whit less than those previously dealt with, will demonstrate their impiety coupled with great ignorance. For if the combination of the parts makes up the whole, and the whole is combined out of the parts, then the whole consists of the parts, and each of them is a portion of the whole.

But this is very far removed from the conception of God. For God is a whole and not a number of parts, and does not consist of diverse elements, but is Himself the Maker of the system of the universe. For see what impiety they utter against the Deity when they say this. For if He consists of parts, certainly it will follow that He is unlike Himself, and made up of unlike parts. For if He is sun, He is not moon, and if He is moon, He is not earth, and if He is earth, He cannot be sea: and so on, taking the parts one by one, one may discover the absurdity of this theory of theirs. 4. But the following point, drawn from the observation of our human body, is enough to refute them. For just as the eye is not the sense of hearing, nor is the latter a hand: nor is the belly the breast, nor again is the neck a foot, but each of these has its own function, and a single body is composed of these distinct parts,–having its parts combined for use, but destined to be divided in course of time when nature, that brought them together, shall divide them at the will of God, Who so ordered it;–thus (but may He that is above pardon the argument [44]), if they combine the parts of creation into one body and proclaim it God, it follows, firstly, that He is unlike Himself, as shewn above; secondly, that He is destined to be divided again, in accordance with the natural tendency of the parts to separation.

---

[44] Cf. Orat. i. 25, note 2.

Against the Heathen (Contra Gentiles)

Section 29

S:29. The balance of powers in Nature shews that it is not God, either collectively, or in parts. And in yet another way one may refute their godlessness by the light of truth. For if God is incorporeal and invisible and intangible by nature, how do they imagine God to be a body, and worship with divine honour things which we both see with our eyes and touch with our hands? 2. And again, if what is said of God hold true, namely, that He is almighty, and that while nothing has power over Him, He has power and rule over all, how can they who deify creation fail to see that it does not satisfy this definition of God? For when the sun is under the earth, the earth's shadow makes his light invisible, while by day the sun hides the moon by the brilliancy of his light. And hail ofttimes injures the fruits of the earth, while fire is put out if an overflow of water take place. And spring makes winter give place, while summer will not suffer spring to outstay its proper limits, and it in its turn is forbidden by autumn to outstep its own season. 3. If then they were gods, they ought not to be defeated and obscured by one another, but always to co-exist, and to discharge their respective functions simultaneously. Both by night and by day the sun and the moon and the rest of the band of stars ought to shine equally together, and give their light to all, so that all things might be illumined by them. Spring and summer and autumn and winter ought to go on without alteration, and together. The sea ought to mingle with the springs, and furnish their drink to man in common. Calms and windy blasts ought to take place at the same time. Fire and water together ought to furnish the same service to man. For no one would take any hurt from them, if they are gods, as our opponents say, and do nothing for hurt, but rather all things for good. 4. But if none of these things are possible, because of their mutual incompatibility, how does it remain possible to give to these things, mutually incompatible and at strife, and unable to combine, the name of gods, or to worship them with the honours due to God? How could things naturally discordant give peace to others for their prayers, and become to them authors of concord? It is not then likely that the sun or the moon, or any other part of creation, still less statues in stone, gold, or other material, or the Zeus, Apollo, and the rest, who are the subject of the poet's fables, are true gods: this our argument has shewn. But some of these are parts of creation, others have no life, others have been mere mortal men. Therefore their worship and deification is no part of religion, but the bringing in of godlessness and of all impiety, and a sign of a wide departure from the knowledge of the one true God, namely the Father of Christ. 5. Since then this is thus proved, and the idolatry of the Greeks is shewn to be full of all ungodliness, and that its introduction has been not for the good, but for the ruin, of human life;–come now, as our argument promised at the outset, let us, after having confuted error, travel the way of truth, and behold the Leader and Artificer of the Universe, the Word of the Father, in order that through Him we may apprehend the Father, and that the Greeks may know how far they have separated themselves from the truth.

Part II - Section 30

S:30. The soul of man, being intellectual, can know God of itself, if it be true to its own nature. The tenets we have been speaking of have been proved to be nothing more than a false guide for life; but the way of truth will aim at reaching the real and true God. But for its knowledge and accurate comprehension, there is need of none other save of ourselves. Neither as God Himself is above all, is the road to Him afar off or outside ourselves, but it is in us and it is possible to find it from ourselves, in the first instance, as Moses also taught, when he said [45]: "The word" of faith "is within thy heart." Which very thing the Saviour declared and confirmed, when He said: "The kingdom of God is within you [46]." 2. For having in ourselves faith, and the kingdom of God, we shall be able quickly to see and perceive the King of the Universe, the saving Word of the Father. And let not the Greeks, who worship idols, make excuses, nor let any one else simply deceive himself, professing to have no such road and therefore finding a pretext for his godlessness. 3. For we all have set foot upon it, and have it, even if not all are willing to travel by it, but rather to swerve from it and go wrong, because of the pleasures of life which attract them from without. And if one were to ask, what road is this? I say that it is the soul of each one of us, and the

---

[45] Deut. xxx. 14.
[46] Luc. xvii. 12.

71

intelligence which resides there. For by it alone can God be contemplated and perceived. 4. Unless, as they have denied God, the impious men will repudiate having a soul; which indeed is more plausible than the rest of what they say, for it is unlike men possessed of an intellect to deny God, its Maker and Artificer. It is necessary then, for the sake of the simple, to shew briefly that each one of mankind has a soul, and that soul rational; especially as certain of the sectaries deny this also, thinking that man is nothing more than the visible form of the body. This point once proved, they will be furnished in their own persons with a clearer proof against the idols.

Section 31

S:31. Proof of the existence of the rational soul. (1) Difference of man from the brutes. (2) Man's power of objective thought. Thought is to sense as the musician to his instrument. The phenomena of dreams bear this out. Firstly, then, the rational nature of the soul is strongly confirmed by its difference from irrational creatures. For this is why common use gives them that name, because, namely, the race of mankind is rational. 2. Secondly, it is no ordinary proof, that man alone thinks of things external to himself, and reasons about things not actually present, and exercises reflection, and chooses by judgment the better of alternative reasonings. For the irrational animals see only what is present, and are impelled solely by what meets their eye, even if the consequences to them are injurious, while man is not impelled toward what he sees merely, but judges by thought what he sees with his eyes. Often for example his impulses are mastered by reasoning; and his reasoning is subject to after-reflection. And every one, if he be a friend of truth, perceives that the intelligence of mankind is distinct from the bodily senses. 3. Hence, because it is distinct, it acts as judge of the senses, and while they apprehend their objects, the intelligence distinguishes, recollects, and shews them what is best. For the sole function of the eye is to see, of the ears to hear, of the mouth to taste, of the nostrils to apprehend smells, and of the hands to touch. But what one ought to see and hear, what one ought to touch, taste and smell, is a question beyond the senses, and belonging to the soul and to the intelligence which resides in it. Why, the hand is able to take hold of a sword-blade, and the mouth to taste poison, but neither knows that these are injurious, unless the intellect decide. 4. And the case, to look at it by aid of a simile, is like that of a well-fashioned lyre in the hands of a skilled musician. For as the strings of the lyre have each its proper note, high, low, or intermediate, sharp or otherwise, yet their scale is indistinguishable and their time not to be recognized, without the artist. For then only is the scale manifest and the time right, when he that is holding the lyre strikes the strings and touches each in tune. In like manner, the senses being disposed in the body like a lyre, when the skilled intelligence presides over them, then too the soul distinguishes and knows what it is doing and how it is acting. 5. But this alone is peculiar to mankind, and this is what is rational in the soul of mankind, by means of which it differs from the brutes, and shews that it is truly distinct from what is to be seen in the body. Often, for example, when the body is lying on the earth, man imagines and contemplates what is in the heavens. Often when the body is quiet[47], and at rest and asleep, man moves inwardly, and beholds what is outside himself, travelling to other countries, walking about, meeting his acquaintances, and often by these means divining and forecasting the actions of the day. But to what can this be due save to the rational soul, in which

---

[47] Cf. Vit. Ant. 34.

man thinks of and perceives things beyond himself?

Section 32

S:32. (3) The body cannot originate such phenomena; and in fact the action of the rational soul is seen in its over-ruling the instincts of the bodily organs. We add a further point to complete our demonstration for the benefit of those [48] who shamelessly take refuge in denial of reason. How is it, that whereas the body is mortal by nature, man reasons on the things of immortality, and often, where virtue demands it, courts death? Or how, since the body lasts but for a time, does man imagine of things eternal, so as to despise what lies before him, and desire what is beyond? The body could not have spontaneously such thoughts about itself, nor could it think upon what is external to itself. For it is mortal and lasts but for a time. And it follows that that which thinks what is opposed to the body and against its nature must be distinct in kind. What then can this be, save a rational and immortal soul? For it introduces the echo of higher things, not outside, but within the body, as the musician does in his lyre. 2. Or how again, the eye being naturally constituted to see and the ear to hear, do they turn from some objects and choose others? For who is it that turns away the eye from seeing? Or who shuts off the ear from hearing, its natural function? Or who often hinders the palate, to which it is natural to taste things, from its natural impulse? Or who withholds the hand from its natural activity of touching something, or turns aside the sense of

---

[48] Supra xxx.

smell from its normal exercise[49]? Who is it that thus acts against the natural instincts of the body? Or how does the body, turned from its natural course, turn to the counsels of another and suffer itself to be guided at the beck of that other? Why, these things prove simply this, that the rational soul presides over the body. 3. For the body is not even constituted to drive itself, but it is carried at the will of another, just as a horse does not yoke himself, but is driven by his master. Hence laws for human beings to practise what is good and to abstain from evil-doing, while to the brutes evil remains unthought of and undiscerned, because they lie outside rationality and the process of understanding. I think then that the existence of a rational soul in man is proved by what we have said.

---

[49] Compare the somewhat analogous argument in Butler, Serm. ii.

Section 33

S:33. The soul immortal. Proved by (1) its being distinct from the body, (2) its being the source of motion, (3) its power to go beyond the body in imagination and thought. But that the soul is made immortal is a further point in the Church's teaching which you must know, to show how the idols are to be overthrown. But we shall more directly arrive at a knowledge of this from what we know of the body, and from the difference between the body and the soul. For if our argument has proved it to be distinct from the body, while the body is by nature mortal, it follows that the soul is immortal, because it is not like the body. 2. And again, if as we have shewn, the soul moves the body and is not moved by other things, it follows that the movement of the soul is spontaneous, and that this spontaneous movement goes on after the body is laid aside in the earth. If then the soul were moved by the body, it would follow that the severance of its motor would involve its death. But if the soul moves the body also, it follows all the more that it moves itself. But if moved by itself [50], it follows that it outlives the body. 3. For the movement of the soul is the same thing as its life, just as, of course, we call the body alive when it moves, and say that its death takes place when it ceases

---

[50] Cf. Plato Phaedr. 245 C-E., Legg. 896, A, B. The former passage is more likely to be referred to here as it is, like the text, an argument for immortality. Athan. has also referred to Phaedrus above, S:5. (Against Gwatkin, Studies, p. 101.)

moving. But this can be made clearer once for all from the action of the soul in the body. For if even when united and coupled with the body it is not shut in or commensurate with the small dimensions of the body, but often[51], when the body lies in bed, not moving, but in death-like sleep, the soul keeps awake by virtue of its own power, and transcends the natural power of the body, and as though travelling away from the body while remaining in it, imagines and beholds things above the earth, and often even holds converse with the saints and angels who are above earthly and bodily existence, and approaches them in the confidence of the purity of its intelligence; shall it not all the more, when separated from the body at the time appointed by God Who coupled them together, have its knowledge of immortality more clear? For if even when coupled with the body it lived a life outside the body, much more shall its life continue after the death of the body, and live without ceasing by reason of God Who made it thus by His own Word, our Lord Jesus Christ. 4. For this is the reason why the soul thinks of and bears in mind things immortal and eternal, namely, because it is itself immortal. And just as, the body being mortal, its senses also have mortal things as their objects, so, since the soul contemplates and beholds immortal things, it follows that it is immortal and lives for ever. For ideas and thoughts about immortality never desert the soul, but abide in it, and are as it were the fuel in it which ensures its immortality. This then is

---

[51] Cp. xxxi. 5, and ref.

why the soul has the capacity for beholding God, and is its own way thereto, receiving not from without but from herself the knowledge and apprehension of the Word of God.

Section 34

S:34. The soul, then, if only it get rid of the stains of sin is able to know God directly, its own rational nature imaging back the Word of God, after whose image it was created. But even if it cannot pierce the cloud which sin draws over its vision, it is confronted by the witness of creation to God. We repeat then what we said before, that just as men denied God, and worship things without soul, so also in thinking they have not a rational soul, they receive at once the punishment of their folly, namely, to be reckoned among irrational creatures: and so, since as though from lack of a soul of their own they superstitiously worship soulless gods, they are worthy of pity and guidance. 2. But if they claim to have a soul, and pride themselves on the rational principle, and that rightly, why do they, as though they had no soul, venture to go against reason, and think not as they ought, but make themselves out higher even than the Deity? For having a soul that is immortal and invisible to them, they make a likeness of God in things visible and mortal. Or why, in like manner as they have departed from God, do they not betake themselves to Him again? For they are able, as they turned away their understanding from God, and feigned as gods things that were not, in like manner to ascend with the intelligence of their soul, and turn back to God again. 3. But turn back they can, if they lay aside the filth of all lust which they have put on, and wash it away persistently, until they have got rid of all the foreign matter that has affected their soul, and can shew it in its simplicity as it was made, that so they may be able by it to behold the Word of the Father after Whose likeness they were originally made. For the soul is made after the image and likeness of God, as divine Scripture also shews, when it says in the person of God[52]: "Let us make man after our Image and likeness." Whence also when it gets rid of all the filth of sin which covers it and retains only the likeness of the Image in its purity, then surely this latter being thoroughly brightened, the soul beholds as in a mirror the Image of the Father, even the Word, and by His means reaches the idea of the Father, Whose Image the Saviour is. 4. Or, if the soul's own teaching is insufficient, by reason of the external things which cloud its intelligence, and prevent its seeing what is higher, yet it is further possible to attain to the knowledge of God from the things which are seen, since Creation, as though in written characters, declares in a loud voice, by its order and harmony, its own Lord and Creator.

---

[52] Gen. i. 26.

Part III - Section 35

S:35. Creation a revelation of God; especially in the order and harmony pervading the whole. For God, being good and loving to mankind, and caring for the souls made by Him,–since He is by nature invisible and incomprehensible, having His being beyond all created existence[53], for which reason the race of mankind was likely to miss the way to the knowledge of Him, since they are made out of nothing while He is unmade,–for this cause God by His own Word gave the Universe the Order it has, in order that since He is by nature invisible, men might be enabled to know Him at any rate by His works[54]. For often the artist even when not seen is known by his works. 2. And as they tell of Phidias the Sculptor that his works of art by their symmetry and by the proportion of their parts betray Phidias to those who see them although he is not there, so by the order of the Universe one ought to perceive God its maker and artificer, even though He be not seen with the bodily eyes. For God did not take His stand upon His invisible nature (let none plead that as an excuse) and leave Himself utterly unknown to men; but as I said above, He so ordered Creation that although He is by nature invisible He may yet be known by His works. 3. And I say this not on my own authority, but on the strength of what I learned from men who have

---

[53] Cf. below, 40. 2.
[54] Cf. Orat. ii. 32.

spoken of God, among them Paul, who thus writes to the Romans[55]: "for the invisible things of Him since the creation the world are clearly seen, being understood by the things that are made;" while to the Lycaonians he speaks out and says[56]: "We also are men of like passions with you, and bring you good tidings, to turn from these vain things unto a Living God, Who made the heaven and the earth and the sea, and all that in them is, Who in the generations gone by suffered all nations to walk in their own ways. And yet He left not Himself without witness, in that He did good, and gave you[57] from heaven rains and fruitful seasons, filling your hearts with food and gladness." 4. For who that sees the circle of heaven and the course of the sun and the moon, and the positions and movements of the other stars, as they take place in opposite and different directions, while yet in their difference all with one accord observe a consistent order, can resist the conclusion that these are not ordered by themselves, but have a maker distinct from themselves who orders them? or who that sees the sun rising by day and the moon shining by night, and waning and waxing without variation exactly according to the same number of days, and some of the stars running their courses and with orbits

---

[55] Rom. i. 20.

[56] Acts xiv. 15.

[57] humin and humon below are read by several mss., and are probably correct as in the original passage.

various and manifold, while others move [58] without wandering, can fail to perceive that they certainly have a creator to guide them?

---

[58] The fixed' stars as distinct from the planets. For the argument, cf. Plato, Legg. 966 E.

Section 36

S:36. This the more striking, if we consider the opposing forces out of which this order is produced. Who that sees things of opposite nature combined, and in concordant harmony, as for example fire mingled with cold, and dry with wet, and that not in mutual conflict, but making up a single body, as it were homogeneous, can resist the inference that there is One external to these things that has united them? Who that sees winter giving place to spring and spring to summer and summer to autumn, and that these things contrary by nature (for the one chills, the other burns, the one nourishes, the other destroys), yet all make up a balanced result beneficial to mankind,–can fail to perceive that there is One higher than they, Who balances and guides them all, even if he see Him not? 2. Who that sees the clouds supported in air, and the weight of the waters bound up in the clouds, can but perceive Him that binds them up and has ordered these things so? Or who that sees the earth, heaviest of all things by nature, fixed upon the waters, and remaining unmoved upon what is by nature mobile, will fail to understand that there is One that has made and ordered it, even God? Who that sees the earth bringing forth fruits in due season, and the rains from heaven, and the flow of rivers, and springing up of wells, and the birth of animals from unlike parents, and that these things take place not at all times but at determinate seasons,–and in general, among things mutually unlike and contrary, the balanced and uniform order to which they conform,–can resist the inference that there is one Power which orders and administers them, ordaining things well as it thinks fit? 4. For left to themselves they could not subsist or ever be able to appear, on account of their mutual contrariety of nature. For water is by nature heavy, and tends to flow downwards, while the clouds are light and belong to the class of things which tend to soar and mount upwards. And yet we see water, heavy as it is, borne aloft in the clouds. And again, earth is very heavy, while water on the other hand is relatively light; and yet the heavier is supported upon the lighter, and the earth does not sink, but remains immoveable. And male and female are not the same, while yet they unite in one, and the result is the generation from both of an animal like them. And to cut the matter short, cold is opposite to heat, and wet fights with dry, and yet they come together and are not at variance, but they agree, and produce as their result a single body, and the birth of everything.

Section 37

S:37. The same subject continued. Things then of conflicting and opposite nature would not have reconciled themselves, were there not One higher and Lord over them to unite them, to Whom the elements themselves yield obedience as slaves that obey a master. And instead of each having regard to its own nature and fighting with its neighbour, they recognise the Lord Who has united them, and are at concord one with another, being by nature opposed, but at amity by the will of Him that guides them. 2. For if their mingling into one were not due to a higher authority, how could the heavy mingle and combine with the light, the wet with the dry, the round with the straight, fire with cold, or sea with earth, or the sun with the moon, or the stars with the heaven, and the air with the clouds, the nature of each being dissimilar to that of the other? For there would be great strife among them, the one burning, the other giving cold; the heavy dragging downwards, the light in the contrary direction and upwards; the sun giving light while the air diffused darkness: yes, even the stars would have been at discord with one another, since some have their position above, others beneath, and night would have refused to make way for day, but would have persisted in remaining to fight and strive against it. 3. But if this were so, we should consequently see not an ordered universe, but disorder, not arrangement but anarchy, not a system, but everything out of system, not proportion but disproportion. For in the general strife and conflict either all things would be destroyed, or the prevailing principle alone would appear. And even the latter would shew the disorder of the whole, for left alone, and deprived of the help of the others, it would throw the whole out of gear, just as, if a single hand and foot were left alone, that would not preserve the body in its integrity. 4. For what sort of an universe would it be, if only the sun appeared, or only the moon went her course, or there were only night, or always day? Or what sort of harmony would it be, again, if the heaven existed alone without the stars, or the stars without the heaven? Or what benefit would there be if there were only sea, or if the earth were there alone without waters and without the other parts of creation? Or how could man, or any animal, have appeared upon earth, if the elements were mutually at strife, or if there were one that prevailed, and that one insufficient for the composition of bodies. For nothing in the world could have been composed of heat, or cold, or wet, or dry, alone, but all would have been without arrangement or combination. But not even the one element which appeared to prevail would have been able to subsist without the assistance of the rest: for that is how each subsists now.

Section 38

S:38. The Unity of God shewn by the Harmony of the order of Nature. Since then, there is everywhere not disorder but order, proportion and not disproportion, not disarray but arrangement, and that in an order perfectly harmonious, we needs must infer and be led to perceive the Master that put together and compacted all things, and produced harmony in them. For though He be not seen with the eyes, yet from the order and harmony of things contrary it is possible to perceive their Ruler, Arranger, and King. 2. For in like manner as if we saw a city, consisting of many and diverse people, great and small, rich and poor, old and young, male and female, in an orderly condition, and its inhabitants, while different from one another, yet at unity among themselves, and not the rich set against the poor, the great against the small, nor the young against the old, but all at peace in the enjoyment of equal rights,–if we saw this, the inference surely follows that the presence of a ruler enforces concord, even if we do not see him; (for disorder is a sign of absence of rule, while order shews the governing authority: for when we see the mutual harmony of the members in the body, that the eye does not strive with the hearing, nor is the hand at variance with the foot, but that each accomplishes its service without variance, we perceive from this that certainly there is a soul in the body that governs these members, though we see it not); so in the order and harmony of the Universe, we needs must perceive

God the governor of it all, and that He is one and not many. 3. So then this order of its arrangement, and the concordant harmony of all things, shews that the Word, its Ruler and Governor, is not many, but One. For if there were more than one Ruler of Creation, such an universal order would not be maintained, but all things would fall into confusion because of their plurality, each one biasing the whole to his own will, and striving with the other. For just as we said that polytheism was atheism, so it follows that the rule of more than one is the rule of none. For each one would cancel the rule of the other, and none would appear ruler, but there would be anarchy everywhere. But where no ruler is, there disorder follows of course. 4. And conversely, the single order and concord of the many and diverse shews that the ruler too is one. For just as though one were to hear from a distance a lyre, composed of many diverse strings, and marvel at the concord of its symphony, in that its sound is composed neither of low notes exclusively, nor high nor intermediate only, but all combine their sounds in equal balance,–and would not fail to perceive from this that the lyre was not playing itself, nor even being struck by more persons than one, but that there was one musician, even if he did not see him, who by his skill combined the sound of each string into the tuneful symphony; so, the order of the whole universe being perfectly harmonious, and there being no strife of the higher against the lower or the lower against the higher, and all things making up one order, it is consistent to think that the Ruler and King of all Creation is one and not many, Who by His own light illumines and gives movement to all.

Section 39

S:39. Impossibility of a plurality of Gods. For we must not think there is more than one ruler and maker of Creation: but it belongs to correct and true religion to believe that its Artificer is one, while Creation herself clearly points to this. For the fact that there is one Universe only and not more is a conclusive proof that its Maker is one. For if there were a plurality of gods, there would necessarily be also more universes than one. For neither were it reasonable for more than one God to make a single universe, nor for the one universe to be made by more than one, because of the absurdities which would result from this. 2. Firstly, if the one universe were made by a plurality of gods, that would mean weakness on the part of those who made it, because many contributed to a single result; which would be a strong proof of the imperfect creative skill of each. For if one were sufficient, the many would not supplement each other's deficiency. But to say that there is any deficiency in God is not only impious, but even beyond all sacrilege. For even among men one would not call a workman perfect if he were unable to finish his work, a single piece, by himself and without the aid of several others. 3. But if, although each one was able to accomplish the whole, yet all worked at it in order to claim a share in the result, we have the laughable conclusion that each worked for reputation, lest he should be suspected of inability. But, once more, it is most grotesque to ascribe vainglory to gods. 4. Again, if each one were sufficient for the creation of the whole, what need of more than one, one being self-sufficient for the universe? Moreover it would be evidently impious and grotesque, to make the thing created one, while the creators were many and different, it being a maxim of science[59] that what is one and complete is higher than things that are diverse. 5. And this you must know, that if the universe had been made by a plurality of gods, its movements would be diverse and inconsistent. For having regard to each one of its makers, its movements would be correspondingly different. But such difference again, as was said before, would involve disarray and general disorder; for not even a ship will sail aright if she be steered by many, unless one pilot hold the tiller[60], nor will a lyre struck by many produce a tuneful sound, unless there be one artist who strikes it. 6. Creation, then, being one, and the Universe one, and its order one, we must perceive that its King and Artificer also is one. For this is why the Artificer Himself made the whole universe one, lest by the coexistence of more than one a plurality of makers should be supposed; but that as the work is one, its Maker also may be believed to be One. Nor does it follow from the unity of the Maker that the Universe must be one, for God might have made others as well. But because the Universe that has been made is one, it is necessary to believe that its Maker also is one.

---

[59] Or, perhaps, "innate, self-evident maxim" (logos phusikos).
[60] lit. "the steering-paddles."

Section 40

S:40. The rationality and order of the Universe proves that it is the work of the Reason or Word of God. Who then might this Maker be? for this is a point most necessary to make plain, lest, from ignorance with regard to him, a man should suppose the wrong maker, and fall once more into the same old godless error, but I think no one is really in doubt about it. For if our argument has proved that the gods of the poets are no gods, and has convicted of error those that deify creation, and in general has shewn that the idolatry of the heathen is godlessness and impiety, it strictly follows from the elimination of these that the true religion is with us, and that the God we worship and preach is the only true One, Who is Lord of Creation and Maker of all existence. 2. Who then is this, save the Father of Christ, most holy and above all created existence[61], Who like an excellent pilot, by His own Wisdom and His own Word, our Lord and Saviour Christ, steers and preserves and orders all things, and does as seems to Him best? But that is best which has been done, and which we see taking place, since that is what He wills; and this a man can hardly refuse to believe. 3. For if the movement of creation were irrational, and the universe were borne along without plan, a man might fairly disbelieve what we say. But if it subsist in reason and wisdom and skill, and is perfectly ordered throughout, it follows that He that is over it and has ordered it is

---

[61] Cf. above 2. 2 and note, also 35. 1.

none other than the [reason or] Word of God. 4.
But by Word I mean, not that which is involved
and inherent in all things created, which some are
wont to call the seminal[62] principle, which is
without soul and has no power of reason or
thought, but only works by external art, according
to the skill of him that applies it,–nor such a word
as belongs to rational beings and which consists of
syllables, and has the air as its vehicle of
expression,–but I mean the living and powerful
Word of the good God, the God of the Universe,
the very Word which is God[63], Who while
different from things that are made, and from all
Creation, is the One own Word of the good
Father, Who by His own providence ordered and
illumines this Universe. 5. For being the good
Word of the Good Father He produced the order
of all things, combining one with another things
contrary, and reducing them to one harmonious
order. He being the Power of God and Wisdom
of God causes the heaven to revolve, and has
suspended the earth, and made it fast, though
resting upon nothing, by His own nod[64].
Illumined by Him, the sun gives light to the
world, and the moon has her measured period of
shining. By reason of Him the water is suspended
in the clouds; the rains shower upon the earth,
and the sea is kept within bounds, while the earth
bears grasses and is clothed with all manner of
plants. 6. And if a man were incredulously to ask,

---

[62] spermatikos

[63] Joh. i. 1.

[64] neuma, i.e. act of will, or fiat.

as regards what we are saying, if there be a Word of God at all[65], such an one would indeed be mad to doubt concerning the Word of God, but yet demonstration is possible from what is seen, because all things subsist by the Word and Wisdom of God, nor would any created thing have had a fixed existence had it not been made by reason, and that reason the Word of God, as we have said.

---

[65] De Incarn. 41. 3.

Section 41

S:41. The Presence of the Word in nature necessary, not only for its original Creation, but also for its permanence. But though He is Word, He is not, as we said, after the likeness of human words, composed of syllables; but He is the unchanging Image of His own Father. For men, composed of parts and made out of nothing, have their discourse composite and divisible. But God possesses true existence and is not composite, wherefore His Word also has true Existence and is not composite, but is the one and only-begotten God[66] , Who proceeds in His goodness from the Father as from a good Fountain, and orders all things and holds them together. 2. But the reason why the Word, the Word of God, has united Himself[67] with created things is truly wonderful, and teaches us that the present order of things is none otherwise than is fitting. For the nature of created things, inasmuch as it is brought into being out of nothing, is of a fleeting sort, and weak and mortal, if composed of itself only. But the God of all is good and exceeding noble by nature,—and therefore is kind. For one that is good can grudge nothing[68]: for which reason he does not grudge even existence, but desires all to exist, as objects for His loving-kindness. 3. Seeing

---

[66] Joh. i. 18, R.V. Marg

[67] epibebeken, see for the sense Incarn. 43. 4, &c.

[68] Plato Timaeus 29 E, quoted also de Incarn. 3. 3. This explanation of Divine Creation is also adopted by Philo de Migratione Abrah. 32 (and see Drummond's Philo, vol. 2, pp. 56, sqq.).

then all created nature, as far as its own laws were concerned, to be fleeting and subject to dissolution, lest it should come to this and lest the Universe should be broken up again into nothingness, for this cause He made all things by His own eternal Word, and gave substantive existence to Creation, and moreover did not leave it to be tossed in a tempest in the course of its own nature, lest it should run the risk of once more dropping out of existence[69]; but, because He is good He guides and settles the whole Creation by His own Word, Who is Himself also God, that by the governance and providence and ordering action of the Word, Creation may have light, and be enabled to abide alway securely. For it partakes of the Word Who derives true existence from the Father, and is helped by Him so as to exist, lest that should come to it which would have come but for the maintenance of it by the Word,–namely, dissolution,–"for He is the Image of the invisible God, the first-born of all Creation, for through Him and in Him all things consist, things visible and things invisible, and He is the Head of the Church," as the ministers of truth teach in their holy writings[70].

---

[69] Plato Politic. (see de Incarn. 43. 7, note).
[70] Col. i. 15-18

Section 42

S:42. This function of the Word described at length. The holy Word of the Father, then, almighty and all-perfect, uniting with the universe and having everywhere unfolded His own powers, and having illumined all, both things seen and things invisible, holds them together and binds them to Himself, having left nothing void of His own power, but on the contrary quickening and sustaining all things everywhere, each severally and all collectively; while He mingles in one the principles of all sensible existence, heat namely and cold and wet and dry, and causes them not to conflict, but to make up one concordant harmony. 2. By reason of Him and His power, fire does not fight with cold nor wet with dry, but principles mutually opposed, as if friendly and brotherly combine together, and give life to the things we see, and form the principles by which bodies exist. Obeying Him, even God the Word, things on earth have life and things in the heaven have their order. By reason of Him all the sea, and the great ocean, move within their proper bounds, while, as we said above, the dry land grows grasses and is clothed with all manner of diverse plants. And, not to spend time in the enumeration of particulars, where the truth is obvious, there is nothing that is and takes place but has been made and stands by Him and through Him, as also the Divine[71] says, "In the beginning was the Word, and the Word was with God, and the Word was

---

[71] Joh. i. 1.

100

God; all things were made by Him, and without Him was not anything made." 3. For just as though some musician, having tuned a lyre, and by his art adjusted the high notes to the low, and the intermediate notes to the rest, were to produce a single tune as the result, so also the Wisdom of God, handling the Universe as a lyre, and adjusting things in the air to things on the earth, and things in the heaven to things in the air, and combining parts into wholes and moving them all by His beck and will, produces well and fittingly, as the result, the unity of the universe and of its order, Himself remaining unmoved with the Father while He moves all things by His organising action, as seems good for each to His own Father. 4. For what is surprising in His godhead is this, that by one and the same act of will He moves all things simultaneously, and not at intervals, but all collectively, both straight and curved, things above and beneath and intermediate, wet, cold, warm, seen and invisible, and orders them according to their several nature. For simultaneously at His single nod what is straight moves as straight, what is curved also, and what is intermediate, follows its own movement; what is warm receives warmth, what is dry dryness, and all things according to their several nature are quickened and organised by Him, and He produces as the result a marvellous and truly divine harmony.

Section 43

S:43. Three similes to illustrate the Word's relation to the Universe. And for so great a matter to be understood by an example, let what we are describing be compared to a great chorus. As then the chorus is composed of different people, children, women again, and old men, and those who are still young, and, when one, namely the conductor, gives the sign, each utters sound according to his nature and power, the man as a man, the child as a child, the old man as an old man, and the young man as a young man, while all make up a single harmony; 2. or as our soul at one time moves our several senses according to the proper function of each, so that when some one object is present all alike are put in motion, and the eye sees, the ear hears, the hand touches, the smell takes in odour, and the palate tastes,—and often the other parts of the body act too, as for instance if the feet walk; 3. or, to make our meaning plain by yet a third example, it is as though a very great city were built, and administered under the presence of the ruler and king who has built it; for when he is present and gives orders, and has his eye upon everything, all obey; some busy themselves with agriculture, others hasten for water to the aqueducts, another goes forth to procure provisions,—one goes to senate, another enters the assembly, the judge goes to the bench, and the magistrate to his court. The workman likewise settles to his craft, the sailor goes down to the sea, the carpenter to his workshop, the physician to his treatment, the architect to his building; and while one is going to the country, another is returning from the country, and while some walk about the town others are going out of the town and returning to it again: but all this is going on and is organised by the presence of the one Ruler, and by his management: 4. in like manner then we must conceive of the whole of Creation, even though the example be inadequate, yet with an enlarged idea. For with the single impulse of a nod as it were of the Word of God, all things simultaneously fall into order, and each discharge their proper functions, and a single order is made up by them all together.

Section 44

S:44. The similes applied to the whole Universe, seen and unseen. For by a nod and by the power of the Divine Word of the Father that governs and presides over all, the heaven revolves, the stars move, the sun shines, the moon goes her circuit, and the air receives the sun's light and the aether his heat, and the winds blow: the mountains are reared on high, the sea is rough with waves, and the living things in it grow, the earth abides fixed, and bears fruit, and man is formed and lives and dies again, and all things whatever have their life and movement; fire burns, water cools, fountains spring forth, rivers flow, seasons and hours come round, rains descend, clouds are filled, hail is formed, snow and ice congeal, birds fly, creeping things go along, water-animals swim, the sea is navigated, the earth is sown and grows crops in due season, plants grow, and some are young, some ripening, others in their growth become old and decay, and while some things are vanishing others are being engendered and are coming to light. 2. But all these things, and more, which for their number we cannot mention, the worker of wonders and marvels, the Word of God, giving light and life, moves and orders by His own nod, making the universe one. Nor does He leave out of Himself even the invisible powers; for including these also in the universe inasmuch as he is their maker also, He holds them together and quickens them by His nod and by His providence. And there can be no excuse for disbelieving this. 3. For as by His own providence bodies grow and the rational soul moves, and possesses life and thought, and this requires little proof, for we see what takes place,–so again the same Word of God with one simple nod by His own power moves and holds together both the visible universe and the invisible powers, allotting to each its proper function, so that the divine powers move in a diviner way, while visible things move as they are seen to do. But Himself being over all, both Governor and King and organising power, He does all for the glory and knowledge of His own Father, so that almost by the very works that He brings to pass He teaches us and says, "By the greatness and beauty of the creatures proportionably the maker of them is seen[72]."

---

[72] Wisd. xiii. 5.

Section 45

S:45. Conclusion. Doctrine of Scripture on the subject of Part I. For just as by looking up to the heaven and seeing its order and the light of the stars, it is possible to infer the Word Who ordered these things, so by beholding the Word of God, one needs must behold also God His Father, proceeding from Whom He is rightly called His Father's Interpreter and Messenger. 2. And this one may see from our own experience; for if when a word proceeds from men [73] we infer that the mind is its source, and, by thinking about the word, see with our reason the mind which it reveals, by far greater evidence and incomparably more, seeing the power of the Word, we receive a knowledge also of His good Father, as the Saviour Himself says, "He that hath seen Me hath seen the Father[74]." But this all inspired Scripture also teaches more plainly and with more authority, so that we in our turn write boldly to you as we do, and you, if you refer to them, will be able to verify what we say. 3. For an argument when confirmed by higher authority is irresistibly proved. From the first then the divine Word firmly taught the Jewish people about the abolition of idols when it said [75]: "Thou shalt not make to thyself a graven image, nor the likeness of anything that is in the heaven above or in the earth beneath." But the

---

[73] Cf. de Sent. Dionys. 23.
[74] Joh. xiv. 9.
[75] Ex. xx. 4.

cause of their abolition another writer declares [76], saying: "The idols of the heathen are silver and gold, the works of men's hands: a mouth have they and will not speak, eyes have they and will not see, ears have they and will not hear, noses have they and will not smell, hands have they and will not handle, feet have they and will not walk." Nor has it passed over in silence the doctrine of creation; but, knowing well its beauty, lest any attending solely to this beauty should worship things as if they were gods, instead of God's works, it teaches men firmly beforehand when it says[77]: "And do not when thou lookest up with thine eyes and seest the sun and moon and all the host of heaven, go astray and worship them, which the Lord thy God hath given to all nations under heaven." But He gave them, not to be their gods, but that by their agency the Gentiles should know, as we have said, God the Maker of them all. 4. For the people of the Jews of old had abundant teaching, in that they had the knowledge of God not only from the works of Creation, but also from the divine Scriptures. And in general to draw men away from the error and irrational imagination of idols, He saith[78]: "Thou shalt have none other gods but Me." Not as if there were other gods does He forbid them to have them, but lest any, turning from the true God, should begin to make himself gods of what were not, such as those who in the poets and

---

[76] Ps. cxv. 4-7.

[77] Deut. iv. 19.

[78] Ex. xx. 3.

writers are called gods, though they are none. And the language itself shews that they are no Gods, when it says, "Thou shalt have none other gods," which refers only to the future. But what is referred to the future does not exist at the time of speaking.

Section 46

S:46. Doctrine of Scripture on the subject of Part 3. Has then the divine teaching, which abolished the godlessness of the heathen or the idols, passed over in silence, and left the race of mankind to go entirely unprovided with the knowledge of God? Not so: rather it anticipates their understanding when it says[79]: "Hear, O Israel, the Lord thy God is one God;" and again, "Thou shalt love the Lord thy God with all thy heart and with all thy strength;" and again, "Thou shalt worship the Lord thy God, and Him only shalt thou serve, and shalt cleave to Him." 2. But that the providence and ordering power of the Word also, over all and toward all, is attested by all inspired Scripture, this passage suffices to confirm our argument, where men who speak of God say[80]: "Thou hast laid the foundation of the earth and it abideth. The day continueth according to Thine ordinance." And again[81]: "Sing to our God upon the harp, that covereth the heaven with clouds, that prepareth rain for the earth, that bringeth forth grass upon the mountains, and green herb for the service of man, and giveth food to the cattle." 3. But by whom does He give it, save by Him through Whom all things were made? For the providence over all things belongs naturally to Him by Whom they were made; and who is this save the Word of God, concerning Whom in

---

[79] Deut. vi. 4, 5, 13.
[80] Ps. cxix. 90.
[81] Ps. cxlvii. 7-9.

another psalm[82] he says: "By the Word of the Lord were the heavens made, and all the host of them by the Breath of His mouth." For He tells us that all things were made in Him and through Him. 4. Wherefore He also persuades us and says[83], "He spake and they were made, He commanded and they were created;" as the illustrious Moses also at the beginning of his account of Creation confirms what we say by his narrative[84], saying: and God said, "let us make man in our image and after our likeness:" for also when He was carrying out the creation of the heaven and earth and all things, the Father said to Him[85], "Let the heaven be made," and "let the waters be gathered together and let the dry land appear," and "let the earth bring forth herb" and "every green thing:" so that one must convict Jews also of not genuinely attending to the Scriptures. 5. For one might ask them to whom was God speaking, to use the imperative mood? If He were commanding and addressing the things He was creating, the utterance would be redundant, for they were not yet in being, but were about to be made; but no one speaks to what does not exist, nor addresses to what is not yet made a command to be made. For if God were giving a command to the things that were to be, He must have said, "Be made, heaven, and be made, earth, and come forth, green herb, and be created, O man." But in

---

[82] Ps. xxxiii. 6.

[83] Ps. cxlviii. 5.

[84] Gen. i. 20.

[85] Gen. i. 6-11.

fact He did not do so; but He gives the command thus: "Let us make man," and "let the green herb come forth." By which God is proved to be speaking about them to some one at hand: it follows then that some one was with Him to Whom He spoke when He made all things. 6. Who then could it be, save His Word? For to whom could God be said to speak, except His Word? Or who was with Him when He made all created Existence, except His Wisdom, which says[86]: "When He was making the heaven and the earth I was present with Him?" But in the mention of heaven and earth, all created things in heaven and earth are included as well. 7. But being present with Him as His Wisdom and His Word, looking at the Father He fashioned the Universe, and organised it and gave it order; and, as He is the power of the Father, He gave all things strength to be, as the Saviour says[87]: "What things soever I see the Father doing, I also do in like manner." And His holy disciples teach that all things were made "through Him and unto Him;" 8. and, being the good Offspring of Him that is good, and true Son, He is the Father's Power and Wisdom and Word, not being so by participation[88], nor as if these qualifies were

---

[86] Prov. viii. 27.

[87] Joh. v. 19; Col. i. 16.

[88] metoche, cf. de Syn. 48, 51, 53. This was held by Arians, but in common with Paul Samos. and many of the Monarchian heretics. The same principle in Orig. on Ps. 135 (Lomm. xiii. 134) ou kata metousian alla kat' ousian theos.

imparted to Him from without, as they are to those who partake of Him and are made wise by Him, and receive power and reason in Him; but He is the very Wisdom, very Word, and very own Power of the Father, very Light, very Truth, very Righteousness, very Virtue, and in truth His express Image, and Brightness, and Resemblance. And to sum all up, He is the wholly perfect Fruit of the Father, and is alone the Son, and unchanging Image of the Father.

Section 47

S:47. Necessity of a return to the Word if our corrupt nature is to be restored. Who then, who can declare the Father by number, so as to discover the powers of His Word? For like as He is the Father's Word and Wisdom, so too condescending to created things, He becomes, to impart the knowledge and apprehension of Him that begot Him, His very Brightness and very Life, and the Door, and the Shepherd, and the Way, and King and Governor, and Saviour over all, and Light, and Giver of Life, and Providence over all. Having then such a Son begotten of Himself, good, and Creator, the Father did not hide Him out of the sight of His creatures, but even day by day reveals Him to all by means of the organisation and life of all things, which is His work. 2. But in and through Him He reveals Himself also, as the Saviour says: "I in the Father and the Father in Me:" so that it follows that the Word is in Him that begat Him, and that He that is begotten lives eternally with the Father. But this being so, and nothing being outside Him, but both heaven and earth and all that in them is being dependent on Him, yet men in their folly have set aside the knowledge and service of Him, and honoured things that are not instead of things that are: and instead of the real and true God deified things that were not, "serving the creature rather than the Creator [190] ," thus involving themselves in foolishness and impiety. 3. For it is just as if one were to admire the works more than the workman, and being awestruck at the public

113

works in the city, were to make light of their builder, or as if one were to praise a musical instrument but to despise the man who made and tuned it. Foolish and sadly disabled in eyesight! For how else had they known the building, or ship, or lyre, had not the ship-builder made it, the architect built it, or the musician fashioned it? 4. As then he that reasons in such a way is mad, and beyond all madness, even so affected in mind, I think, are those who do not recognise God or worship His Word, our Lord Jesus Christ the Saviour of all, through Whom the Father orders, and holds together all things, and exercises providence over the Universe; having faith and piety towards Whom, my Christ-loving friend, be of good cheer and of good hope, because immortality and the kingdom of heaven is the fruit of faith and devotion towards Him, if only the soul be adorned according to His laws. For just as for them who walk after His example, the prize is life everlasting, so for those who walk the opposite way, and not that of virtue, there is great shame, and peril without pardon in the day of judgment, because although they knew the way of truth their acts were contrary to their knowledge.

Printed in Great Britain
by Amazon